Boc Training:

Power strategies to unleash the force of great training

By the Experts at

Tortal Training

Contents

Introduction: Why Your Training Department Is a Profit Center, Not a Cost

"We just hired a new training development company," the CEO of a retail company was heard to say recently, "and we're going to be paying a much higher cost for our training than ever before. It better work."

It's easy to appreciate that executive's concerns. After all, increasing expenditures always require careful consideration. Yet we disagree with that executive in two important aspects . . .

- **First,** training is not a cost, it is an investment, as we will explain in a moment.
- **Second,** you can't just sit back and hope training will work. You have to take steps to make sure it does.

Why Training Is a Profit-Making Investment, Not a Cost

When you pay your electrical bill or insurance, that is a cost, because those expenses will probably not pay you a quantifiable return on your money. Paying for training is different. It is making an investment that can, and actually must, pay you a sizable ROI, for reasons like these . . .

- **Every dollar you invest in effective sales training will pay you back many times over** - For example, you can train retail salespeople to close more sales, to increase the amount of each sale they make, to upsell, to add new products to orders, and more. It is reasonable to expect that after training, your salespeople will be able to sell at least 10% more. And you can do the math. If your company currently has $20 million in annual sales, for example, you can sell $2 million more by introducing training that costs much less than that. Let us restate, you are making a profitable investment, not spending money on something that doesn't deliver any return to you.

- **Every dollar you invest in customer service training will pay you a similar return -** If your company does that same $20 million in annual sales and your customer retention rate drops five percentage points in one year, that could mean you have lost about $1 million in sales. Yet the right kind of customer service training can turn that problem around. When you consider that you can invest a relatively small amount of money in training to achieve $1 million more in annual sales, you quickly realize that your training department is a profit center, not an expense.

Plus, Great Training Rewards You with Improved Employee Retention

Well-trained employees are happier and therefore less likely to leave you. Because they are more confident and do their jobs better, they will generate higher profits too. And you will have to replace fewer of them.

It's another example of why your training department is a profit center, not a drain on your resources. Provided, of course, that you change your thinking and act accordingly to get the largest ROI from your training.

What Kind of Training Pays You the Biggest Returns?

The quick answer to that question is, "Good training." But it is not as simple as that. To achieve the biggest ROI, you and your training designers should answer these questions . . .

- What larger **business goals** would we like our training to achieve?
- Which **employees** should we train if we want to reach those goals?
- Which of those employees' **skills and tasks** will we address through training?
- Can we talk to employees who are **currently handling those tasks** and understand what they do and what is not working? (Note that this is part of the DACUM, or "Design a Curriculum" approach to training design.)
- What can we **measure** before and after training to be sure we have "moved the needle" and brought about real change?
- Who are our employees, where are they, and what is the **most effective way** to deliver training to them?

In Summary . . .

Do you have to pay for training? Of course you do. Can it be expensive? Of course it can. But thanks to new training technologies that include training on mobile devices, there are more ways than ever before to keep costs low.

When you do that and unlock new profits by training at the same time, you have hit the "sweet spot" that makes training profitable.

Part One: To Succeed, You Need to Train

Why You Are Paying for Training . . . Whether You Know It or Not

Every company pays for training. You can either pay for it up front or pay for it through poor results at many times the cost of doing it right. People don't think about it this way, but they should.

Here is a story about a company where a lack of training was costing $1.68 million a year.

Our CEO once directed a team that took over the operations of a chain of nine floor covering stores, a business that was doing $12 million in annual sales. The overall goal was to show that training and merchandising tools could increase profits. The average profit margin on products sold was 34%. Our team knew they could improve that with the right kind of training.

They used a two-part strategy. First, they introduced a more sophisticated merchandising program that included a pricing model, supported by a new store design that communicated the message, "lower pricing" to customers. Second, they trained salespeople to use the tools and focus on solving customers' problems by focusing more on their needs and helping them find real value vs. simply a low price.

As a result, the margin increased from 34% to 48% - a 14% improvement. In that $12 million company, the result was a $1.68 million increase in gross profit dollars plus increased sales. The improvement in profit was demonstrable. The reality is that the true differentiator was the training. If the team had simply changed out the merchandising without doing the training, there would have been a much smaller impact.

Another way to look at it is that for years, a failure to train was costing that company $1.68 million a year in gross profit. The cost of training for this company was in essence $1.8 million per year, because they didn't spend any money on training. You see, every company pays for training. They can either pay for it up front or they pay for it through poor results at many times the cost of doing it right.

Are you too paying for training without knowing it? Let's take a close look at just how that could be happening to you.

Lost Opportunity: You Could Train Staff to Close More Sales

Let's say that your staff should be closing 40% of sales, but currently they are only closing 30%. That means you are losing 25% of potential sales; if your company is doing $10 million in annual sales, you are losing $2,500,000.

With training, increasing a close rate from 30% to 40% is a reasonable expectation. It can mean training staff how to be more polite, listen better, present products more effectively – and ask for the order. It is very, very doable. And if you are not doing it, you are paying for training without even realizing it.

Which is more costly, losing $3 million in sales or investing in training?

Lost Opportunity: You Can Train to Improve Employee Retention

Losing employees is costly. According to a study by the Center for American Progress, the cost of replacing a worker who earns between $30,000 and $50,000 a year is 20% of annual salary, or about $10,000. (If you're losing employees who earn more than $50,000, replacing each of them will cost you even more.)

Let's assume that you have 250 employees and that your annual turnover rate is 30%. So you're losing 75 employees a year and spending $750,000 to replace them.

(You'll also be losing money by paying unemployment benefits, losing sales during the time their jobs are not covered, and more, but let's not figure that in.)

What if you did a better job of training employees and cut your turnover rate by 5%, from 30% to 25%? That is also very doable. That 5% improvement will pay you back more than you expect. If you have 250 employees, you will be losing only about 60 workers a year, not 70, a saving of about $100,000 a year.

Incidentally, the link between training and retention is well documented. Well-trained employees are happier and therefore less likely to leave. And because they do their jobs better, you will have to fire and replace fewer of them.

Which is cheaper - having a high turnover rate that costs you $100,000 a year, or investing in training?

Lost Opportunity: You Can Train Salespeople to Sell Just a Little More on the Average Ticket

Let's assume that your average customer spends $25 on each visit to one of your locations. Through training, you can increase that average ticket to $28. Your staff can learn to refer customers to other products, upsell, and apply other simple strategies.

Let's further assume that you have 400,000 customer transactions a year. If you can train your salespeople to increase ticket size from $25 to $28, you will increase annual sales from $10 million to $11,200,000.

Which is cheaper, losing $1,200,000 in sales or investing in training?

Lost Opportunity: You Can Train to Improve Customer Retention

If your company does that same $10 million in annual sales and your customer retention rate drops five percentage points, that means you have lost $500,000 in sales. Yet the right kind of training in areas likes sales and customer service has been shown to retain many more customers. Again, it is "doable." And the result can be a big improvement in profitability.

Which is cheaper, losing $500,000 worth of customers a year or training?

Let's Review

You pay for training, one way or another. Every company pays for training. You can either pay for it up front or pay for it through poor results at many times the cost of doing it right.

Your company results are affected by the quality of the training your company provides. Investing in training upfront is going to provide you a 10x or greater return on your training dollar.

Additionally, training is the safest investment you can make. If you spend more money in advertising, it may or may not be effective in bringing customers to your business. Training is about improving results with the customers you already have coming to your business.

Every business is different, but how much is poor training costing you? How could investing in training upfront improve your profits?

Those are critical questions to ask in our highly competitive world of business. In the pages that follow in this book, you will discover many answers to them.

Align Your Training Goals with Your Higher Business Goals

"It's not enough to teach knowledge, skills, or behaviors just for the sake of it. Training must connect to big-picture, company-wide objectives. Team members and leaders have to ask, `What do we need to be able to do so we achieve our business goals?` and `How will we measure and show the impact of training on performance?'"

— "4 Training & Development Trends for 2016" by Shannon Leahy, UnboxedTechnology.com

There are really two kinds of training. The first and most basic centers on teaching employees to improve their performance of required skills and tasks. The second kind does that too, but produces far more transformational results, because it also teaches skills and behaviors that align with larger company initiatives and goals.

Here's an analogy that demonstrates the point. First think of a golf caddy as a trainer. That caddy can walk the course and hand his golfer one club at a time and say, "This is the best club for this shot." That might improve the golfer's game. But what if the caddy added a higher level of information by giving perspective on the overall layout of the hole, the potential hazards in the path and even a strategy for playing the entire course?

Similar lessons apply in many settings. Do you want your son or daughter's piano teacher to only teach the mechanics of pushing down a key, or to give an overview of a piece of music? If you are hiring a landscaper for your yard, do you want to discuss only one plant, or do you want to collaborate on an overall, transformational plan.

Given choices like those, of course you prefer the bigger picture. But how do you do that in planning your company training? Here are some important steps to take.

Define Your Most Important Objectives and Keep them in Mind

For example, are you striving to create a company known for delivering superlative customer satisfaction? That is a great objective, but reaching it means defining specifics that can get you there – what you would like your training to achieve.

For example, you could plan to train your phone reps to resolve 90% of all complaints during customers' first calls. Or to train those reps to deliver the kind of care that gets 90% of callers to report on post-call surveys that they are "extremely satisfied." When you define goals, you can design training that achieves them.

Another way of stating this principle is, "begin with the end in mind." That means understanding the bigger vision of what you would like your organization to become, then defining specific training steps that can get you there.

Break Down the Silo Walls

Trainers often are brought into different company sectors and encouraged to stay in them. They might teach skills for servicing or installing products, providing customer service, preparing food, or selling on the retail floor. But what if your trainers thought outside the silos and delivered valuable learning that resulted in improvements across your entire organization?

One way to reach this objective is to initiate discussions between your training team and the people who create marketing and advertising, manage your supply chain, oversee your online presence, and more. The more disciplines you invite into the process, the more likely it becomes that your training team will find ways to make your training more encompassing and effective.

Don't Create Training in a Vacuum

Whether your training team works in-house, or you use an outside training development company, engage them in conversations about company quarterly reports, trade publications, company whitepapers, news stories about your organization, press releases, and all the other pertinent documents you can provide. In sum, do all those materials suggest any untapped opportunities to align your training specifics with larger goals and initiatives?

Tie Your Training to Measurable Metrics

It is essential to develop a set of clear metrics to measure before and after training. It is the only way to understand what your training has accomplished and how much closer you are to meeting your goals.

Here are some suggestions for developing metrics that don't just gather data, but reveal deeper progress:

- **If your vision is to become a leader in customer service and retention,** you can survey customers before and after your training about their overall satisfaction with their last purchase, the likelihood they will recommend you to other customers, and other factors.
- **If you want to gain maximum value from a limited time offer (LTO) and offer training to support that goal,** your goal could be XX% of sales change among employees who took the training. Measure and report on those results after the training has been delivered.
- **If you are implementing HR training** in an effort to increase employee retention and become an "employer of choice" for job-seekers, you can measure retention rates before and after training and survey employees on metrics like, "I see a clear career path if I remain employed" or, "I understand the criteria that my supervisor and company use to evaluate my performance and progress in the company."

How to Create Training that Boosts the Bottom Line

Most business leaders know that effective training builds more consistent performance among employees, improves customer service, reduces the amount of time that managers spend training new employees, and provides other benefits that impact the bottom line.

But do those same businesspeople also understand just how much a company's overall profitability will grow when a comprehensive program of training is put into action? In many cases, they don't. Here's a case study that gives some food for thought for companies that would like to quickly realize significant improvements in their bottom line.

Case Study: A Restaurant Chain You Know

Several years ago, a major national restaurant chain hired Tortal Training to perform a comprehensive analysis of their training programs for new hires and front-line employees. Before working with Tortal, most training there was being delivered by restaurant managers who had to take time away from their other duties to conduct one-on-one training or run training classes.

Tortal designed and implemented a comprehensive eLearning program. One year after the program began, profits had already increased in dramatic ways:

- At restaurants where 80% of employees had completed the eLearning training, overall business had increased by 4%.
- At restaurants where 50% or fewer of the employees had completed the training, business had increased too, but by 1.4%.

Now let's crunch some numbers. Each of those restaurants does about $2 million of business every year. So using that as a baseline, we see that restaurants that had generated 4% more business had made $16,000 more in just one year. In contrast, the restaurants that had achieved 1.4% growth had generated $2,800 in more business.

If you roll out those numbers further, you will see that over a five-year period, the restaurants that trained 80% of their employees would see an increase of $80,000 in new business, compared to $14,000 in companies that had trained 50% of their workers. But in reality, the revised training would generate even a bigger ROI, because:

- **Business growth is cumulative.** Even if a business grows at a rate of 4% every year, that percentage is built on a bigger profit base. So even if the growth rate holds steady, the number of new dollars earned each year will increase.
- **More efficient operations lead to greater profits and growth.** In a restaurant setting, managers who are freed from training responsibilities can invest more of their time running their restaurants. The same principle applies in most businesses. And as we know,

better-trained employees are more efficient, sell more, and generate increased profits.

- **Retention rates among well-trained employees have been proven to be higher than for employees who are not well-trained.** And as every company executive knows, the cost of hiring and training new employees is very high.

Training is a "Must Have," not a "Nice to Have"

How much would your company's profits increase if you were able to increase your annual business by 2%, 4%, 6% or more, and then keep building on those gains? If you don't crunch the numbers, you could underestimate just how big the impact will be on your bottom line. But after you take out a pencil and paper and add things up, you will see that better training has the power to dramatically increase profits in both the short and long term.

Why Failing to Train Your Employees Costs a Lot More than You Think

Please take a moment to think about this conversation that took place between a CEO and his director of training.

The CEO said, "What if we spend all this money training our staff and they leave us?" And the head of training replied, "What if we don't train them and they stay?"

The point of this adage is that if you spend a lot of money and the people you trained leave, that is not great. But if you don't train them and they stay, it costs you a lot of money.

Early in his career when our CEO worked for CCA Global Partners, he supervised operations at a number of flooring stores that practiced a hiring philosophy that seemed logical. The company routinely hired salespeople who had worked at other flooring retailers, and then didn't train them. The assumption was that experienced salespeople were "pretrained." Training them would be costly and superfluous.

That assumption might have made sense, but it was flawed. The fact that those salespeople had experience didn't mean that they came armed with the best selling skills. So, our CEO and his team developed a blended program of live and eLearning that taught the comprehensive selling skills that the company needed. We trained salespeople on the products they were selling, on how to increase the size of the average order, on how to explain to customers what to expect when their new flooring was installed, and more.

The performance of the experienced people we trained was dramatically better than the performance of experienced people who were allowed to "learn on their own." For every $750,000 in sales made by salespeople we trained, the "learn on their own" salespeople generated only $400,00 in sales, or only about 60% of what trained employees did. Another way of looking at it? Untrained employees contributed about 60% of what the trained employees did against margin (the amount of money they generated after subtracting the cost of commissions, the cost of goods sold, the cost of processing credit cards and other expenses).

And the advantage becomes even greater when you consider the additional costs of employment that include benefits, Social Security taxes, the cost of a desk and a phone, and other expenses.

In Tortal's years of analyzing training results, we have seen time and time again that the ROI on training is dramatically greater than most company executives believe it will be. In simple terms, if a trained worker becomes 100% productive and an untrained worker is only 60% productive, you are losing $40,000 in value on every $100,000 of business you conduct.

And here's another statistic that should catch your attention. When you look at the amount of money that each employee contributes after commissions (the "contribution margin"), properly trained salespeople generate something on the order of $122,000 more for every $1 million in sales that your company makes. And when you tally those gains across a salesforce of five, 10, or more employees, you easily see that the gains are significant.

Why Trained Employees Generate More Income

There are many reasons. Trained salespeople . . .

- Close more sales
- Generate larger average sales
- Sell fewer products at discounted prices, and more products at list price
- Make fewer mistakes
- Sell the right products, reducing the cost of returns and product replacements
- Build customer relationships that result in more repeat business
- Generate more positive reviews online
- Increase your Net Promoter scores
- Help keep morale and productivity high among all your employees, because people don't like to work with untrained people who don't know what they are doing

There are many more reasons why trained employees contribute more to the bottom line. Even if you have a company that attracts a small volume of walk-in traffic and only a small number of customers come through your door, for example, trained salespeople will increase profits for you. Even if you do not increase the number of customers you attract, your business will still be up if you train your retail salespeople to sell each customer just a little bit more, to make higher margins.

Training Is Not Just for Salespeople

Before he came to Tortal Training, our CEO was once responsible for creating a program that trained flooring installers the basics of customer service, such as explaining to customers exactly what to expect during the installation process. Thanks to that program, he took the percentage of customers who said they would not buy from that company again from 13% down to less than half a percent.

In Closing . . .

Not training is hugely expensive . . . far more expensive than training. In your company, we urge you to look for all the opportunities where proper training can dramatically increase profits, reduce waste and provide an outsized ROI for every training dollar you spend. If you start to look, you will find many more opportunities than you expect.

To Cultivate Today's Younger Workers, Invest in Training

Copious research documents the fact that Younger Generations like to learn. After all, they grew up attending schools and college; learning is part of the way they interact with the world.

One major study from Gallup, "How Younger Generations Want to Work and Live," reports these findings:

- **60% of Younger Generations** say that the opportunity to learn and grow on the job is extremely important. In contrast, only 40% of Baby Boomers feel the same way.
- **50% of Younger Generations** strongly agree that they plan to remain in their jobs for at least the next year. That might sound like a big percentage, but 60% of members of all other groups plan to stay in place for at least a year. Baby Boomers and others are planning on sticking around, while Younger Generations are weighing their options.

Findings like those document that Younger Generations are more likely to be engaged and to stay on their jobs if they can learn. Yet not all training takes place in a traditional classroom or corporate learning center. Here are some forms of training that appeal strongly to Younger Generation employees:

- **Bite-sized training on mobile devices.** We have observed that Younger Generations especially like training that is delivered to them on their phones. Even more so, they like training that is delivered in short sessions - the kind they can complete while at lunch, on break, or even at the gym.

- **Mentoring relationships with supervisors.** Gallup found that 60% of Younger Generations feel that the quality of the people who manage them is extremely important. With that in mind, your training for new employees can set up mentoring, not reporting, relationships between them and strategic managers. Explain how often check-ins and job reviews with their managers will happen, and what they will cover.
- **Being part of an energized and innovative team.** This is a bit of a contradiction, but at the same time Younger Generations think of themselves as individualist entrepreneurs, they also expect to be part of a great team. Letting Younger Generations get to know their teammates during training, and fostering a sense of team/group identity, can help convince them that they have joined the right organization.

Yes, training is important to Younger Generations. But think of it as more than a chance to teach skills. Younger Generations are the most energized, skilled and capable generation ever to enter the workforce. Train them well and they will become your organization's brightest future.

How to Cultivate a Culture of Learning in Your Organization and In Yourself

Great things happen in companies where executives inspire people to learn. To name just a few . . .

- **An enhanced ability to compete in the marketplace,** because people discover and apply the best information, solutions and ideas
- **More effective leadership,** because executives who love to learn inspire others to perform on a much higher level
- **Improved job retention,** because the work that everyone does becomes more stimulating and engaging
- **Enhanced operations,** because people aren't required to do things . . . they want to try out the newest solutions and ideas

How can you cultivate a culture of learning and enjoy more of those benefits?

Become a Lifelong Learner Yourself – and Talk about It

It might work to say to people, "Go find out about the latest trends in our industry." But people are inspired to do that when company leaders are lifelong learners themselves. In other words, great learning leaders model the kind of learning behavior they would like to inspire in others. Then they actively share their discoveries in meetings and in casual encounters with people.

The more excited you become about what you are learning, the more people will follow suit. One effective approach is to start meetings by talking about something you have learned, and then asking others to contribute too. Another strategy is to start book groups where employees read and discuss important new books; provide the books and hold the sessions during company hours, not lunch hours, to reinforce the idea that learning is a "must do," not a "nice to have" activity.

Open the Doors and Seek Information in New Places

When you stop to think about it, you are surrounded by people who can help everyone in your company learn. They include vendors, executives at other companies, members of professional organizations, and more. You can learn a great deal from companies in other sectors that are targeting the same customers you are – in other words, competing for the same dollars. How are they marketing, delivering customer service, and more?

To stimulate this kind of learning, create task forces that are charged with the responsibility of visiting other companies, attending conferences, reading business books, and then reporting back about the solutions and ideas they have discovered. One powerful suggestion is to have groups of employees evaluate your competitors and then present their findings to you.

The more you integrate learning with work, the more energized your organization becomes.

Let Employees Step out as Company Experts on What They Have Learned

When employees have learned a lot about a topic, find ways to let them share their expertise with everyone in your organization. You can encourage them to blog about what they know, write articles in company newsletters, and lead training sessions.

Those steps inspire your most enthusiastic learners to learn even more, inspire everyone to identify and master areas of learning that interest them, and further build a company culture where learning is a priority.

Create a Personal Development Plan for Each Employee

Instead of only conducting performance reviews, empower the process by creating a personal development plan for every employee in your organization. Discuss specific areas for growth and learning that they would like to investigate, then bring the process to life by adding specific target dates for learning.

Then get together with each employee monthly to review progress. We are very big advocates for this process, because we have seen how powerfully it works to develop people. When people understand what they have to do in order to advance in your company, they are more motivated to learn, excel and serve as role models. Why review learning and growth only once a year?

The Critical Importance of Training During Onboarding

The days and weeks after employees start at your company represent a time of unique opportunity. Can you teach them new systems and skills? Of course you can. But have you also stopped to consider all the other important goals you can reach during the onboarding period? To name just a few, you can . . .

- Grow and encourage adoption of your culture
- Get new hires to understand, promote and believe in your brand
- Sow the seeds for outstanding customer service
- Cultivate the kind of spirit and energy that customers will value and love
- Hear creative ideas from new employees who have a fresh perspective
- Build retention by proving that your company is a great place to work
- Set up communication channels with new hires that will improve operations throughout your company

Those are only a few of the opportunities you have during employees' first weeks at your company. But how can you take advantage of them? Here are eight approaches that work.

1. Start by Having a Well-Defined Onboarding System

Many companies just wing it, with negative results. Still other companies see onboarding as little more than filling out forms, setting up company email accounts and showing new employees to their desks. Because new hires start their jobs without a deeper understanding of what is expected of them, they make mistakes that quickly become costly habits that must be corrected later on.

Many problems can be avoided if you set up a structured onboarding system that functions as high-level training. On their start days, new hires can meet individually with HR representatives to fill out forms, for example, and then meet as a group to watch videos and learn about your company, its brand and its values. After lunch, they can be trained in the basic skills their jobs demand; watching training videos, engaging in work simulations and working alongside current employees can work well to reach those goals. And after day one, they should attend regular follow-ups to address problems and reinforce basic concepts and skills.

The operative strategy is to clearly define ahead of time exactly the skills and behaviors you need, and to create a concise mini-curriculum that tracks to them.

2. Set Up Genuine Mentoring Relationships between New Hires and Successful Current Employees

Remember, mentors' goals should not be to get new hires to imitate what they do, or even to adhere to company systems. Their purpose is to discover what new employees would like to accomplish, and to help them reach those goals. In short, mentoring is not about the mentors or strictly about your company, but about the employees who are being coached.

3. Find Ways to De-Layer and Free Up Communications

Invite new employees to brainstorming sessions where their new ideas are collected, posted, discussed— and put into action when appropriate. Also consider setting up de-layered systems—like virtual suggestion boxes on your company intranet—where employees at all levels can present suggestions directly to top company executives. If employees can only submit ideas to their immediate managers, you have created a communication structure that carries a risk of demotivating front-line and entry-level personnel; just one supervisor who stifles new ideas can do great damage to your company.

4. Don't Do Training on the Cheap

One thing is for certain: if you are only handing out employee handbooks and having new employees fill out withholding forms, you are missing out on some great opportunities. If you can train every new retail salesperson to sell just 10% more on every order, for example, that could result in hundreds of thousands of dollars' worth of new business company-wide, maybe even more. Or if you can set up mobile-based training that sends out pings to remind employees to use specific skills they learned in training, you could increase your training ROI dramatically. The lesson? Spending a little more to deliver great training is a money-maker, not a cost.

5. Within Your Budget, Customize Training for Each Employee

Even "standardized" training can be enriched by creating individualized training elements for each new employee. You can evaluate the skills of your new hires during training and address them directly, for example, or help employees overcome anxiety about performing certain parts of their new jobs. Investing just a little time to give training extra value can go a long way toward getting new employees up to speed faster.

6. Stress and Reinforce Your Mission Statement, Vision Statement and Strategic Company Plan

The onboarding period is a highly effective time to share the big picture about your company and to get employees to buy into your most important goals and priorities. Instead of waiting for employees to discover these critical priorities, start talking about them soon after new hires come on board.

7. Consider Creating a Career Plan for All New Employees

You won't want to do this for seasonal or short-term employees. But for employees whom you would like to stay with you for the long term, consider sitting down with each of them to create individual career-development plans that spell out what they need to do to be promoted within your organization. You could say, for example, that all retail salespeople can apply for management training after six months of employment, or that your company will provide technical training to help them move into their desired career path at your company.

Millennials, especially, are more likely to stay with your company for the long term if they know the ropes and understand what it takes to build a long-term relationship with your organization.

8. Evaluate Whether You Are Acting like a Great Employer

This is something you should always do, not only when you are training a new class of employees. So take the time now to benchmark your company climate, benefits, quality of work/life balance and other factors against other companies. Unless you have the best of everything, you cannot expect your employees to commit their hearts and minds to working with you for the long term.

You see, retention starts with you, not with your employees. Unless you commit your efforts to becoming an "employer of choice" - a company that people talk about and would love to work for - you are damaging your profits, operations and ultimately, your success.

Part Two: Critical Strategies for Training Success

"I wish they'd told me how to deal with the most common complaint I hear from customers, but it never came up in training."

"As soon as we got back onto the selling floor, we saw that we hadn't really learned any tools to do our jobs better."

If you have ever gotten comments like those after investing time and money in training, you'll be pleased to know that you can avoid them by allowing employees to play a bigger role in planning their own training.

Here are some simple questions that can dramatically improve both the results of your training and your ROI.

Question One: "What would you like to learn in training?"

This open-ended question is so simple that some companies forget to ask it. They seem to think they already know what employees need to learn, so why ask? Our advice is, go ahead and ask. The answers you get might not all be usable, but there will be some nuggets of high-value, critically important topics that your training needs to cover. The people who are designing your training – whether your in-house training department or an outside training company – need to pay attention.

Question Two: "What is the biggest challenge that you face on the job?"

This question is not open-ended, but the answers it triggers can be extremely useful as you plan your training topics and curriculum. If there is a question that your phone reps hear every day but cannot answer, for example, shouldn't that be covered in your training?

It's a powerful question for another reason too, because it can uncover issues that training cannot completely solve. If your salespeople are losing sales because customers say that it takes too long to receive their orders or that product quality is not good, those are issues that need to be addressed outside the training stream.

Question Three: "What specific processes and steps do you perform as you do your job?"

This question, which lets trainees explain all the sub-steps of what they do, can uncover specific tasks and activities that your training can improve most powerfully. If you own an appliance store and you want to train your delivery and installation personnel to provide better service to customers, for example, you will be reminded that there is more to delivering a new stove than simply wheeling it into a customer's house and hooking it up. Your delivery people need to find the delivery location, park the delivery truck, unpack the stove, discard packing materials, navigate delivery through different kinds of residences, answer customer questions, demonstrate how the appliance operates after it has been installed – and engage in a number of specific sub-steps.

If you review those steps and discuss them with your future trainees, you will discover that some of them have the potential to yield greater process improvements than others do. That's another way of saying that you can leverage greater value by bringing more focus to your training.

"Everyone is different and as a result may have something special to bring to the table. Let them know how their personalities and unique strengths support your organization. Take advantage of these differences."

– "Embrace Uniqueness of Your Employees," by Shep Hyken, Shep Hyken's Customer Service Blog

Could it be that better training results when you train to individual employees' strengths, not their weaknesses? Could it also be that the best training happens when you get different people to act in different ways – not the same way?

Our friend Shep Hyken, a leading expert in the field of customer service training, thinks so. Shep, who presented one of our Breakthrough Thinking in Training Webinars, has even created a simple training exercise that allows people to discover and start to use their unique strengths.

We like it and we want to tell you about it. It can save you time and help you achieve better results, faster. Here's how he describes his exercise on his blog:

- **Break** your training class into small groups of five or six people.
- **Explain** that you want each group to assemble a collection of 26 objects – one for each letter of the alphabet. (*Examples:* A bottle of aspirin for the letter "A," a book for the letter "B" and

so on.) Invite trainees to find the objects in their pockets, purses, or briefcases.

- **Declare** a winner when the first group finds all 26 objects.

Big Power in a Little Exercise

Shep points out that this exercise, simple though it may be, teaches some important lessons to trainees:

- **First,** they discover that working as a team produces better results than working individually.
- **Second,** because instructions are "loose," trainees come up with unique and highly individual approaches to solving the problem, discover their own strengths, and see that those strengths are valued.
- **Third,** individual trainees discover that their very different backgrounds and strengths enabled their teams to come up with superior results.

In other words, the exercise helps trainees discover and accept their individual strengths and also conveys the fact that your organization welcomes and values people as individuals.

Seven Ways to Keep Your Employees Engaged
in Training

Have you ever gotten comments like these after
one of your training programs has ended?

- "I doubt that I'll actually use any of these
  concepts when I get back to my job."
- "How much can I be expected to learn
  when I sit in a chair and have somebody talk
  at me for an entire day?"
- "The training never addressed the biggest
  frustration I deal with on the job every
  day."
- "The sales trainer was full of energy, but we
  really needed practical selling strategies,
  not hype."

Statements like those – and we have all heard
them – could be telling you that you delivered
substandard, poorly designed training. But they
might be telling you something else about your
employee training activities . . .

You failed to engage your learners

Engagement is the key to effective training! And
how do you make your training engaging? Let's
look at seven critical principles.

Critical Concept #1: Focus on a Small Number of Concepts

Cordell Riley, President of Tortal Training, believes
that one of the first steps to effective learning
development is to focus on only a small number of

key concepts to teach. He points out that when companies assemble a team and start to design a training program, they tend to list a dozen or more topics that they plan to cover. In other words, they want their training program to teach everything.

The result, he points out, is "like expecting people to drink water from a fire hose." And he is right. Ample research has shown that trainees usually absorb only between one and three key concepts, then they shut down mentally and stop learning.

There is a more effective way. Cordell points out that you might not have to teach all your most critical concepts during a single program of training, because you can bring trainees back for follow-up training, text them new concepts to use, and more. Training is not "once and done," it should be an ongoing part of working for you.

Furthermore, learners' mental focus stays strong for fewer than 20 minutes. Which is why you need to apply Critical Concept #2 . . .

Critical Concept #2: Provide a Variety of Engaging Training Activities

Variety, it is often said, is the spice of life. It is the spice of good training too. So make your training more energizing by mixing in a variety of training formats that can include . . .

- Games
- Motivational talks and lectures
- Videos
- Interactive exercises

- Work simulations
- Break-out sessions
- Actual on-the-job working experiences

Yet there is more to great training than simply providing variety. Make sure to apply Critical Concept #3 too . . .

Critical Concept #3: Use the VAK Learning Styles Model to Make Your Training "Stickier"

The VAK model means offering training experiences that are:
- **Visual**, such as illustrations, graphs, videos, highlighted text and even cartoons.
- **Auditory**, such as voiceovers and narrations.
- **Kinesthetic**, involving physical movement. (Get your trainees out of their chairs and get them moving around the room, or even outside the building.)

Because most people prefer to learn in one of these three styles, mix and match them to ensure your training will be better absorbed by everyone. Above all, resist the temptation to throw learning content at your trainees by giving them a page of text to read or playing a long, recorded audio conveying the same information. Mix things up!

The good news is that the technology you need to create high-quality videos is already right there on your computer or phone, allowing you to economically author engaging videos and audio files you can embed in your training courses.

The Tortal Learning Management System's Course Authoring Tool also lets you insert videos that you have found on YouTube and Vimeo into your courses, wherever you choose. Another great idea? If you create videos of your own, post them to YouTube or Vimeo. You can then update them and link to them, without needing to redo your entire course.

Yet even "mixing things up" might not do enough to energize your learners through a long day of training. Apply Critical Concept #4 too . . .

Critical Concept #4: Plan Your Training Day around Circadian Rhythms

Your trainees will experience energy highs and lows at different times of the day, according to their internal, biological clocks. Have you ever noticed that your energy tends to sag immediately after lunch, for example, or that you have the most energy at the start of the day? If so, you have observed circadian rhythm at work.

Evan Hackel, our CEO, has written about the importance of scheduling "high learning" sessions at the start of the day, or just before lunch. After lunch, you can schedule interactive activities that allow people to tap into each other's energy. Then at the end of the afternoon, you can schedule tests and evaluations that let people show what they have learned. Tortal Training's Learning Development Team can help you design a day of learning that synchs with natural circadian rhythms, and dramatically improves the effectiveness of your training.

Yet training is not a "one way street" in which employees learn and the company reaps all the benefits. To reward them, move on to Critical Concept #5 too . . .

Critical Concept #5: Reward and Recognize Learners with Fun Learning Experiences

Taking a day of training is not easy, and trainees who are working hard like to feel that their efforts are being noticed and appreciated by your company. Let them know that you appreciate their efforts! You can express that appreciation in a variety of ways that can include:

- **Graded quizzes** that allow trainees to demonstrate their new knowledge . . . and be called out and recognized for scoring well.
- **Fun and funny experiences** that break up the day. A karaoke session, scavenger hunt, or other energizing experience can add energy to a long day in the classroom. Just make sure that these activities synch with training goals – if not, they risk becoming frivolous.
- **Prizes** and fun stuff. Don't overdo it, since some people might think they are corny. But no matter what your trainees say, handing out fun and funny rewards can help keep them engaged.
- **Surprise visits** from your company leaders. A brief, energizing visit from your CEO or president can provide variety and demonstrate that training is important.

- **And give out certificates** to employees who have completed a day of training. You will be surprised how many employees will put them up in their work areas and see them as a source of pride.

And to make sure your training is addressing the questions that your learners are thinking about, apply Critical Concept #6 too . . .

Critical Concept #6: During Training, Let Trainees Tell You What They Would Like to Learn

This Critical Concept takes training to a higher level by addressing the common post-training complaint, "The training never actually taught me to deal with the problems I face on the job."

So while training is taking place, ask questions like these:

- "What would you like to learn today?"
- "What's on your mind that we still need to explore?"
- "What frustrations are you dealing with every day on the job . . . and can we find solutions to them today?"

You can appoint one trainee to write down on a whiteboard the issues that emerge from those questions, and then initiate a group discussion about them. Or you could have trainees anonymously write down and submit their suggestions for topics to discuss and have the training leader have discussions around them.

And then when trainees do tell you what they would like to learn, make an immediate effort to provide focused training that delivers. You can, for example, bring in a department head to lead a discussion, get a vendor on a video call to answer questions, and deliver in other ways. People ask . . . and you deliver.

And here's another way to build more engaged learning, perhaps the most important of all, Critical Concept #7 . . .

Critical Concept #7: Tell Your Trainees the Benefits of Taking Your Training

Be sure to spell out a meaningful WIIFM ("What's In It For Me") benefit that lets your trainees understand a clear reason to take your training. Note that Evan Hackel, our CEO, has written about this concept in his book, *Ingaging Leadership: 21 Steps to Elevate Your Business.*

So when you announce a training program, be sure to trumpet a meaningful, proven benefit, such as:

- "Learn effective, no-pressure ways to **get every customer to buy 25% more** . . . and see your commissions soar."
- "In just an hour of training, you will learn to **fill out your sales reports** in five minutes or fewer, so you can spend more of your time selling."
- "This training will **double the size of the tips you receive** from every table of patrons you serve in our restaurant."

- "You will learn three proven ways to **increase your monthly commission** by 35%."

The more you demonstrate the WIIFM, the more motivated people will be to engage fully in your training and master the skills that help them – and your organization – perform at a higher level.

In-House Training vs. Taking Classes: Which Will Teach Your Employees What They Need?

You need to teach a specific skill to a group of your employees. You just found a course at a local college that seems to fill the bill. Or perhaps your industry association offers classes that might be just right.

Should you enroll your employees in those classes or develop a training program of your own? Let's look at some of the considerations to keep in mind.

First, Pinpoint the Skills You Need to Teach

If you need to teach employees to use a particular software program or to use your new cash registers and you can find a course that focuses specifically on teaching those skills, that course might provide good value and get the job done.

On the other hand, if you need to teach a more complex matrix of skills that are needed to perform a job, it will probably be more effective – and in the end, more cost-effective – to bring in a training developer who can help you define the skills that you need to teach, and then to design a curriculum for them. So consider the job and the skills you need to teach and make the best choice.

Second, Review the Content of the Courses You Are Considering

What exactly do they teach? What percentage of their course units and lessons will be applicable to the jobs and the employees you are training? And what percentage will not apply?

Also look at the biography of the instructor who is teaching the course. Does that background tell you that he or she will teach skills that will apply to your employees and to your company? If so, the course might offer you good value.

Third, Consider the Timeframe

If you need to teach a finite set of skills for a group of employees only once, it might be more efficient and economical to have them take a course at a local community college, online, or through a professional organization. It might also be efficient to bring in an expert or consultant to work with your employees for an afternoon or a day. But if you envision that you will continue to teach the same knowledge to employees over a period of months or years, developing a true training program could offer you better results and better ROI.

Fourth, Consider Your Company's Branding and Unique Value

Chances are that your company is unlike others – better than your competitors. If so, it could be worth investing more money and time to develop training that reflects your brand, company culture, and unique way of doing business.

Fifth, Remember that New Course Design Options Are Available to You

A member of Tortal Training's Learning Development team can explain a number of flexible training options that can teach the skills you need at a cost that works for you.

In Summary . . . Take Responsibility for Delivering Engaging Training

Have you ever been in a meeting in your training department where someone said, "It was a really good training program . . . why didn't anybody like it?"

If you have been in a meeting where a comment like that was made, your training department is blaming employees for a problem that you, not they, caused. The problem? You failed to deliver interesting employee training that engaged your learners!

Invest in Training that Gets Results, Not Training that is Frivolous

Sometimes it is hard to tell the difference. Let's take a look at two professional trainers. Let's call them Joan and Jack.

How Joan and Jack Are Similar

Both Joan and Jack are energetic trainers who get their audiences laughing. They will both do whatever it takes – using props or quacking or asking trainees to do silly things – to illustrate a concept or get everyone engaged. And when trainees leave at the end of the day, they feel energized and happy.

How Joan and Jack Are Different

A few weeks after training is over, the performance of the people who trained with Joan has really improved. The performance of the people who trained with Jack hasn't changed at all. They went back to "business as usual" the moment training was over.

In other words, Jack's training is frivolous. Joan's isn't, because it gets results.

How to Avoid Wasting Money on Frivolous Training

- **Define outcomes and make sure your trainer can reach them.** Do you want your salespeople to contact 25% more new prospects? Do you want the people who deliver and install appliances for your store to give true "white glove" treatment to customers? Or do you want your hotel front-desk staff to delight guests with exceptional service? Your trainer should explain his or her plans to break those processes down into individual steps and address them directly through training.

- **Help your trainer know who your trainees are.** A good trainer will want to know about their ages, prior experience, educational level, current jobs, and all other factors that can be leveraged to engage them more fully in training. A concerned trainer will also want to be aware of any factors that might cause them *not* to engage.
- **Work with your trainer to develop meaningful metrics.** If you work together to define what you will measure after training is completed, chances are good that your training will accomplish much more, because its goals are well defined.
- **Monitor sessions and make sure that training stays on track.** If you are a company training director or a member of senior management, you might not want to attend sessions, because your presence could put a damper on trainees' ability to relax and learn. If that is the case, ask a few trainees to check in with you at lunchtime or other breakpoints to tell you whether the trainer is hitting the benchmarks you created. If not, a quick check-in with the trainer can often get things back on track and avoid wasting time and money.

It's All About Getting Your Money's Worth and Getting Results

If you are a training director who wants to record serious results from serious training, it's important to work closely with professional trainers who don't only entertain, but educate. That's the difference between training that's frivolous and training that offers a good ROI on your investment.

How much does it cost to breathe fresh life into an under-performing training program? Is it even worth trying, or do you need to discard what you have and start designing all over again from the beginning?

Many companies assume that it cannot be done without incurring enormous expenses. But that is often not the case. In fact, dramatic improvements can often be achieved by making simple changes. Here's a case study that proves the point.

The Problem: People Weren't Invested, Training Wasn't Delivering

Back in 2014, a franchised national restaurant chain had a training program that wasn't delivering results. Only 25% of franchisees were using the training. Employees disliked it. And even worse, training was doing little to increase customer satisfaction levels. So Tortal started to ask questions. Here are some of the comments we heard from trainees:

- "Lessons are repetitive."
- "The training gives information, but doesn't teach skills."
- "I can't take time away from my job to complete the long lessons."
- "Modules don't work well together; they're just not well integrated."
- "The eLearning is taking too much time."
- "Lessons are not engaging."

Tortal analyzed the training curriculum, and then we made some changes. We:

- **Reordered lessons** to cover the most important skills and concepts first.
- **Eliminated and reduced** repetitive and redundant portions of lessons, which reduced by as much as 25% the amount of time required to complete each module.
- **Made lessons more engaging** by incorporating games, drag-and-drop exercises, and other interactive content.
- **Created quizzes** for trainees to compete at the end of each module.
- **Enlivened lessons** by using video layovers and two narrators instead of one.
- **Displayed the objective** of each module clearly on all slides so that trainees knew what they are learning and why.
- **Installed a "Next Lesson" button** on the last slide of each module to encourage trainees to move ahead on their own.
- **Made all training materials available** in Spanish as well as English.

Results Achieved

Overall learner seat time was reduced by 25%-40% and more importantly, 67% of customers reported much higher satisfaction levels.

Always Tell Trainees What's in it for Them

All of us at Tortal Training are proud of our CEO Evan Hackel. He just wrote a new book, *Ingaging Leadership: A new approach to leading that builds excellence and organizational success* and we're all talking about how wise and useful it is.

Let's explore one of Evan's principles that can offer a big payback to trainers everywhere.

Be sure to communicate the "What's In It for Me" (WIIFM) when launching training

Evan writes, "People are more likely to read communications or act on them when they perceive a clear and immediate benefit from doing so."

That makes sense, doesn't it? Few people are eager to take part in training (or any other company activity) when the only incentive is, "You have to finish this training by the end of the week, so log in now." But if you trumpet a clear WIIFM, participation and enthusiasm soar.

You can make that happen with communication strategies like these:

- **When announcing a new program of sales training,** say something like, "You are going to close a lot more sales, because salespeople in other locations closed 40% more sales in the first month after taking this training."
- **Before training personnel to use a new company intranet or communication hub,** say "You are going to gain 90 minutes a day that you are now wasting by reading and sending emails . . . what will you do with all that extra time?"
- **Before training store managers to set up a new inventory management system,** say, "You'll keep your store open longer and sell

more because you'll never again have to close your doors to take inventory."

- **Before training regional offices to use a new suite of marketing materials,** say, "You'll see incoming customer calls surge to 30, 40 or more a day . . . that's what happened in Des Moines and Tallahassee, and it can happen for you too."

Don't Avoid Making Trainees a Little Uncomfortable

In a Breakthrough Ideas in Training webinar that Anthony Amos gave for us at Tortal, he made a comment that we've been thinking about ever since . . .

> "Good training coaches people to move through discomfort."

The more we think about that comment, the more we realize how wise Anthony is. After all, discomfort is one of the main reasons people silently resist training . . .

- **Sales trainees** learn your company's strategies and scripts for structured selling . . . but some never admit that they feel uncomfortable about "asking for the buy" and closing sales.
- **Some mature trainees** who are returning to the workforce might be reluctant to admit that they feel insecure about using new technologies.
- **Executives** in your leadership training programs take part in workshops that encourage them to work closely with other departments . . . but some of them secretly feel defensive about sharing too much Information with the heads of other divisions.
- **Some of the phone representatives** who you are training to make cold sales calls never admit they hate to pick up the phone and call people they don't know.

Dealing with Discomfort

Before you can overcome discomfort, you have to find ways to uncover where it lies. Here are some effective ways:

- **Start asking for "mood feedback" as soon as training begins.** Asking a question like, "everybody good with that?" or, "anybody got a problem with that?" consistently through training can set up an atmosphere that encourages trainees to open up about any areas of discomfort. If you keep the mood lighthearted and fun, trainees will be more likely to say what is on their minds.
- **Anticipate and deal with possible "hot button" issues when designing your training.** If you think about who your trainees are and what you would like them to learn, you can often identify areas of discomfort ahead of time and teach to them.

Effective Coaching Techniques for Areas of Discomfort

- **Use simulations.** If a trainee for a calling center job says that she fears dealing with angry customers, let her handle two or three simulated calls from dissatisfied customers. (Other trainees can play the part of the callers.) Once she sees that she can handle those calls well, she will gain the confidence she needs.
- **Use videos in your training.** If you can show employees dealing with situations or issues that you expect will cause trainees discomfort on the job, you can proactively train employees to perform better.

- **Let trainees break into small sub-groups to discuss what they are learning.** Trainees who are reluctant to air fears or concerns before a room full of other trainees are often willing to share their feelings in small groups of their peers. One good technique is to ask each group to appoint a leader to collect comments and then report them to the entire training class.
- **Consider using anonymous feedback.** You can ask trainees to anonymously write down their areas of discomfort on index cards or have them text the training leader. Once those comments are collected, your trainer can talk about them openly with the entire group.
- **Be respectful of trainees' feelings.** You want to keep the mood light but resist the temptation to poke fun at trainees' fears. If a trainee opens up about something that is on his or her mind – something that is a concern – part of a trainer's job is to discuss the issue respectfully and carefully.

Part Three: Winning Ways to Deliver Great Live Training

Critical Details and Logistics to Consider for Your Live Training Day

Big concepts are not the only thing you need to create successful training programs. Getting all the small things right – all the "moving parts" is also essential.

Let' say you've booked a room for your training session. You've ordered coffee, tea, water, and a table of snacks. Of course, you've made sure that the projector and sound system will work. So all the bases are covered, right?

Maybe yes, maybe no. Because the fact is, there are a lot of "moving parts" in any live training session. Paying attention to even the smallest of them can help assure that your day of training will be effective, memorable, motivating, and much more.

Pick the Right Seating Arrangement

Here are some configurations to consider:

- **Banquet-style seating,** where attendees sit at round tables spread around the training room, works well for training groups of 30 or more.

  Benefit: Attendees will already be in groups and there is no need for people to move around for breakout activities.

  Downside: Half the people at each table need to turn and twist in order to see the presenter. Because trainees tend to sit with people they already know and like, your trainer might need to mix things up by assigning tables to trainees by putting table numbers on their nametags, or have trainees change tables when breaking out into groups.

- **Theater-style seating,** where attendees sit in auditorium-style rows, can accommodate very large groups of 100, 200 trainees or even more. It works well when your presenter wants to deliver a big or motivational message.

Benefit: This layout focuses the attention of trainees on what the presenter has to say, by slightly limiting their ability to interact with each other.

Downside: Be sure to consider the training sessions that will follow a theater-style training session. If trainees will need to break out into small groups, you might want to move later training sessions in the day into another room with banquet-style seating, send them in small groups to different rooms, or make other accommodations.

- **Seminar-style seating,** where trainees sit in a U-shaped formation of chairs with the presenter in front of them, works well in smaller groups of up to 20 trainees.

Benefit: Focuses the attention of the group on what the trainer has to say and encourages group discussion.

Downside: If you are planning a full day of training, it is best to plan to move trainees into other configurations as the day progresses, since sitting seminar-style can get tiring in the long haul.

Offer the Right Food and Snacks

This is especially important when training starts in the early morning. Of course you or your planner will provide coffee, tea and bottled water, but the selections that you make beyond that can affect your trainees' ability to focus and get the most from training.

Opinions differ on what to offer, but the best thinking today holds that it is smartest to steer trainees away from sugary breakfast items – which can cause energy highs followed by energy crashes – by offering fruits and (if they are in your budget) healthy breakfast cereals like granola and protein-rich selections like eggs and breakfast meats.

Consider Circadian Rhythms when Planning Your Training Day

People tend to have high energy levels first thing in the morning, settle down slightly and become attentive by late morning, then become sleepy after lunch. With a little thought, you can plan accordingly.

One option: Because trainees can tend to "nod off" immediately after lunch, schedule breakout sessions, interactive training exercises and other energizing activities immediately after lunch instead of lecture presentations. Steer away from lectures where information is delivered one-way.

If Possible, Pick Training Rooms with Natural Light

It's not always possible. But if you have sat in training sessions in rooms with exterior windows, you know that training in natural lighting usually works better because people feel more energized and positive.

Tip: Post-lunch training sessions when people are likely to be sleepy can become deadly in dark interior or basement rooms.

Allow Adequate Breaks to Check Phone Messages and Emails

If you're training a group of new employees, they might not need to check too often for incoming new messages – only about once an hour for personal messages. But if your trainees are your current executives, managers or salespeople, allowing more frequent breaks will let them focus more closely on your training.

Tip: Encourage current employees to "triage" incoming messages by having their clients, administrative support staff and others send them text alerts – which are hard to miss – when an important message needs immediate attention.

How to Maximize the Benefits of Classroom
Training

Are you about to embark on a lengthy process of
migrating your older training materials onto
computers, tablets, or smartphones? Are you sure
that you really need to?

Did you know that instructor-led classroom training
is still the most popular form of training? It's true,
even today when training is increasingly delivered
on mobile phones and tablets. According to
statistics from the Association for Talent
Development, 70% of all training programs in the
U.S. were conducted in classrooms in 2014. We are
willing to bet that at least 60% of all training
programs are still conducted that way today.

Why Classroom Training Still Rules

- **Speed of development.** You can create a
  curriculum and have it tested and running in a
  matter of weeks, not the months it takes to
  develop computerized or training that is
  delivered on mobile devices.
- **Ease of development and lower cost.** In many
  cases, non-technical executives in your
  organization can design and launch classroom
  training without the assistance of computer
  programmers, IT people or other specialists.
- **Flexibility.** Once your classroom materials are
  ready to go, they can be used for training large
  groups of hundreds of employees, small groups
  of a dozen – or anything in between. And if a
  training unit or lesson isn't working, you can

simply replace it without getting bogged down with technological problems.

Is There a Downside?

Classroom training presents very few disadvantages, provided it is expertly designed. The key to success is to make sure that training remains interactive and engaging – not a static experience where one person stands in front of a group and lectures.

Strategies for Keeping Classroom Trainees Involved and Engaged

If you have attended a classroom training program that worked well, chances are you took part in activities like these that offered a lively variety of experiences:

- **Quizzes** that allow participants to score their skills or take part in in other self-assessments.
- **Live surveys,** which can now be conducted live using a variety of apps.
- **Breakout sessions,** where participants meet in groups to discuss topics or generate questions that are then brought back to the entire group.
- **Videos** that offer depictions of the skills that are being taught, company profiles, and other content.
- **Visits to company offices and facilities** where trainees can learn about company operations first-hand.
- **Feedback and Q&A sessions,** offered at regular intervals during training, can introduce new topics for discussion, add value, and keep sessions lively.

- **Role-playing and demonstrations,** where trainees take on the roles of customers, clients or other stakeholders while other trainees play the roles of company employees.

Plan Your Training Day around Energy Highs and Lows

"The Ideal Work Schedule, As Defined by Circadian Rhythms," an article by Christopher M. Barnes in *The Harvard Business Review*, explores the energy peaks and valleys that most people experience through the course of a day. The author writes that it is important to consider those biological rhythms when planning employees' work schedules . . .

"Humans have a well-defined internal clock that shapes our energy levels throughout the day: our circadian process, which is often referred to as a circadian rhythm because it tends to be very regular."

To summarize his points . . .

- Most people reach their first energy peak of the day a few hours after the start of the workday, or at about 10:00 A.M.
- That energy peak lasts about two hours, until lunchtime.
- Energy levels then fall after lunch, hitting bottom at around 3:00 P.M.
- Energy levels then begin to rise, hitting the final peak of the day at about 6:00 P.M.

The information he provides about our "internal clocks" can also help learning designers plan training days where learners can absorb the most information possible.

Planning Training to Synch with Biological Rhythms

After reading that summary, it might be tempting to think that the most logical approach to planning a training day would be to schedule "low-energy" activities during low-energy times of the day and "high-energy" activities at times when energy is peaking.

But as training designers know, that can invite problems. If you turn down the lights and show a 30-minute video right after lunch, for example, chances are pretty good that people will nod off. In fact, low-energy times are often the best times to get trainees out of their chairs and dark classrooms to take part in work simulation exercises, group breakout sessions, and games.

High-energy times, like the two hours before lunch, are often great times to schedule high-content learning experiences that require trainees to be seated, like panel discussions, talks by invited speakers and interactive exercises.

If you are a training professional, you already know how challenging it is to create a high-performing day of training. It takes experience, intuition, the ability to match lesson content to trainees, the skill to create learning that is engaging, and many other skills. But when you get your training just right, both you and your trainees know it. Training design is both an art and a science.

Include Experiential Learning

Research has shown as much as 75% of all learning takes place when people engage in activities. Training is simply more effective when people engage in experiences rather than reading a training manual, looking at a spreadsheet displayed on a screen or engage in other static activities.

Some examples of experiential learning include:

- **Storytelling -** Ask trainees to write a story describing how they used what they have already learned in training. They can then read what they wrote to the training class and discuss.
- **Work simulations –** Stop the course and ask the trainees to demonstrate what they learned. Then proceed.
- **Break-out sessions -** Have trainees divide into sub-groups to discuss concepts or simulate work situations. They can then report back to the course manager and resume.

Even if your training is being delivered on mobile devices or in your company training center, you can still offer experiential learning features that improve trainees' retention of key concepts.

Make Sure Your Training Sessions are the Right Length

What is the ideal length for a training session?

"Short!" one sales trainer told us. And he's right, because trainees shut down and stop learning when sessions run too long.

"Just the right length," another trainer said. When we asked him what that meant, he explained, "It depends on the information you are presenting, how you are delivering it, who your trainers and trainees are, and lots of other factors."

The funny thing is, they are both right. Sessions should ideally be as brief as possible, but these considerations come into play.

What Is Your Delivery System?

As a general rule, "The smaller the delivery device, the shorter lessons should be." Individual training sessions can take an hour or more if people are in big groups. If trainees are completing training on remote computer terminals, lessons can run to 30 or 45 minutes. And if your learners are training on mobile phones, lessons as short as five minutes have been shown to work well.

Where Does Each Training Unit Fit into Your Overall Plan?

If you write down all the skills and information that you want your trainees to take away, you will see that some topics can be taught quickly, while others require more time. When planning a day of sales training, for example, you might want to start your day with a 30-minute motivational session, then follow up with two one-hour focused skill-building sessions – one before lunch and another after. Then in the weeks that follow live training, you can follow up with weekly 30-minute online modules to reinforce key concepts. If you look for it, you will discover that there is an internal rhythm in your training curriculum that can tell you how long each component needs.

What Are the Optimum Ways to Teach Your Topics?

Some concepts can be taught best through interactive online lessons. Others come to life in live training sessions where trainees break into groups and simulate job experiences. Some learning comes alive with videos. For more complex leadership training, it sometimes works best to create teams of trainees and give them real work to do in your business over time.

Creating the right structure for your training curriculum is both an art and a science. An experienced training development company can be your best partner as you plan a curriculum that delivers your learning in just the right formats in the right doses, at the right time.

An Art and a Science . . .

There is no doubt that training design is both an art and a science. An experienced training development company can often save time, money and miscues by suggesting training solutions that have been proven to work.

Get More from Training by Assigning the Right Homework

If you want to hear people groan when a day of training is ending, say "Here's your homework for tomorrow."

Maybe that's because the word "homework" brings back so many unpleasant memories from school. Yet the right kind of homework can be motivating, not discouraging.

A Motivational Way to Use Homework in Training

"The Kind of Homework that Helps Coaching Stick," an article that Prof. Monique Valcour wrote for the March 3, 2015 *Harvard Business Review,* offers some advice that we like about the role that homework can play in coaching professionals to learn, improve and find a path to advancement in your organization. Prof. Valcour is professor of management at EDHEC in France, one of Europe's top business schools.

"In order to give your employees meaningful homework," Prof. Valcour writes, "lay the groundwork by stepping out of the directing role and into a listening and learning role. By asking open-ended questions, listening actively, and engaging respectfully with your employees, you build the trust and rapport that is the lifeblood of effective coaching. As you gain greater insight into your employee's thinking, motivations and interests, you'll be better able to challenge and support him or her with homework that stimulates learning and development."

Encourage Trainees to Think about Advancement

Prof. Valcour believes that the right kind of homework motivates employees to further their career development. She suggests having trainees consider questions like these and bring their answers back to their coaches:

- "How do you think you can add greater value to our organization?"
- "Are there specific roles in the company that you would like to know more about?"
- "Are there specific projects here that you would like to work on – and how would they help you reach your career goals?"

So, Is Homework Taboo?

Used in the right way, it can enhance your training programs. We like Prof. Valcour's value-adding strategy of encouraging trainees to think about career development during training.

This is a powerful lesson that can help you achieve a much higher ROI in all your training programs.

It's tempting to think that employees will like your training because it gives them a chance to kick back and get away from their desks. But the fact is, training could be causing conflicts like these for your trainees:

- "I get 100 emails before lunch every day, some of them critically important . . . what am I supposed to do, just disappear during training?"
- "I'm onboarding three new associates this week . . . and I'm expected to go sit in a classroom all day long?"
- "I'm hoping to close a big sale next week . . . and my company expects me to go to another state for training?"

You get the idea. Training can cause conflicts for executives, middle managers, salespeople, front-line staffers, and just about everyone else. If you don't address the problem, you're only causing people to resent training before it even begins, and to resist it even more after it starts. But there are ways to resolve the conflict.

Ask Employees to Help Design the Training that Will Work Best for Them

Do your middle managers really want to travel away from their home offices? Do your salespeople want to leave their territories and sit in meetings without immediate access to incoming phone calls?

There are alternatives. Videoconferencing can let you run a virtual group training class for only an hour a day, for example. Interactive online training can allow salespeople, customer service people, and other staffers to fit training in and around their other work. And you can mix and match different delivery systems to minimize the conflict between learning and work.

Help Trainees Stay on Top of Work During Live Sessions

Have you ever been in training classes where attendees are secretly checking their mobile devices and hoping nobody will notice? Everybody becomes irritated – the trainer and the trainees too. But there are some strategies that can prevent the problem:

- **"Decriminalize" the use of mobile devices.** Your trainer can simply tell trainees that they may keep their phones in sight, right where they are sitting, and that they may keep an eye on emails, texts and incoming calls.
- **Schedule frequent breaks.** You can tell trainees that there will be a 10-minute communications break at the end of every hour of training. You can also provide different kinds of communication breaks at different times in your training; there will be no checking phones during the first 30-minute live morning presentation, for example, then more frequent breaks through the afternoon. Just be sure to communicate how those breaks will work, so

trainees will know what to expect and can concentrate more completely on training.

- **Let trainees prioritize their communications.** If you encourage trainees to set up alerts for their most critical communications, they will engage more fully in training. If one of your salespeople is expecting an important phone call from a potential customer, for example, she can encourage that client to send a text instead of calling or emailing. She can also have a support person in her office send her a text alert as soon as the customer calls. The key is to anticipate and plan for important communications, not react after they have happened.

Don't Just Announce Training . . . Plan It

If you have read between the lines in this section, you have seen the underlying message that designing effective training is an interactive process between training designers and trainees. The more you engage your trainees in planning, the more effective it becomes.

Part Four: Delivering Great Training at Conferences and Off-Site Meetings

Plan Off-Site Training that Resonates with Your Company Culture

"I flew to attend a weekend of off-site sales training," says a man who works for a large company that sells footwear that it both imports from other countries and manufactures domestically. "We are a traditional company overall. I mean, we are a family-owned business headquartered in the Midwest and have a long history of doing business in a rather conservative way.

"But as soon as I walked into the first training session of the day, I honestly thought I had wandered into an event that was being held by another company, not ours. The trainer was hyper, over-energized, strident and LOUD. And he wasn't talking about our products or even our industry. To be sure I was in the right place, I had to look around the room to identify people I knew.

"After that first surprising experience, things settled down as we went into afternoon sessions, and things got better. But what on Earth were our company leaders thinking when they lined up that first trainer? I can only conclude that they had made a serious mistake or been sold a bill of goods by some outside company. It was a terrible way to kick off our weekend of training."

There Is Little We Can Add to That . . .

Even if you want to energize your trainees, be sure to plan training that synchs with your company culture and norms. Chances are that your employees know what your brand stands for, how you do business, and your company mission and values. So be sure to work with a training development company that either understands who you are, or that is willing to learn.

Select a Great Conference Venue

How can you choose the best location and venue for your conference or off-site training?

The question to start with is . . .

Where will your trainees be traveling from in order to attend?

If all your trainees will be coming from one region of the country, it becomes easier to choose a venue for your conference. Simply explore hotels and conference centers in your region, negotiate your best package, and you are on your way to deciding on a good venue.

If on the other hand your trainees will be coming from a wider region, or even from across the country or from other countries, one major concern is how far important "hub" airports are located from the facility you decide to use. ("Hubs" are airports that are served by large airlines; in many cases, they can be accessed by those airlines without the need for connecting flights.)

If Your Attendees Will Fly Long Distances, What Hubs Are Best to Be Near?

Unfortunately, there is no one answer to that question, because choosing the best hub for your convention to be near depends on two factors:

1. The regions of the country your attendees will be coming from

2. The airlines they will probably be using to come to your conference

Fortunately, there is a website, TripPlus.com, that offers a directory of airport hubs that are served by different airlines.

Even more fortunately, event planners at hotels you are considering can offer the transportation information you will need as you make your plans. If you call a hotel, ask to speak to its event and conference planner and explain where your trainees will be traveling from, they will be able to offer advice and information.

We know one company that called a hotel's event planner, explained where its trainees would be coming from, and that event planner said, "You shouldn't hold your event here . . . you should hold it in Denver because of airline routes."

Hospitality professionals are often as honest as that. Many of them know that if they provide you with the best advice and information, you will be inclined to use their services again when future needs arise.

Also be sure to ask about transportation between the conference center and the airport. Many hotels offer complimentary shuttle bus service to groups that have booked blocks of rooms. That convenience can serve as an added incentive that influences your employees to come to your event.

Factors that Can Lower Room Rates

One thing for certain is that if you simply provide your attendees with a toll-free number or a Website address and encourage them to reserve their own rooms, they are going to end up paying more than they should, which can of course discourage them from attending. Plus, allowing your employees to book rooms on their own can lead to further complications if they decide to make reservations not directly with the hotel, but with popular online discount travel companies.

Here are some steps that can avoid those difficulties and keep the costs of hotel rooms low:

- **Book a block of rooms well ahead of time.** Your employees can then call the hotel, give the name of your company, and make reservations conveniently.
- **Book all rooms for the same number of days.** If you can tell the hotel, for example, that all the members of your group will be checking in on Tuesday and departing on Friday, that will result in lower rates.
- **As early as possible, have your trainees confirm their plans to attend.** You can then provide the hotel with a close-to-accurate count of the rooms you will need. The earlier you can provide the facility with a firm count of attendees, the more leverage you will have in negotiating reduced rates. Also encourage your employees to sign up for the convention you will be having next year. The earlier you can determine the attendance you will have at future conferences, the more leverage you will

have to negotiate better hotel rates in the future.

- **Book your conference at a time when the hotel is likely to have the most vacant rooms.** There are slow months and busy periods, often tied to seasons and holidays. If you talk to venues and explain that you would like to book a conference at a time when they will have blocks of open rooms available, you will be in a position to negotiate for low prices.

What Features and Extras Should Your Venue Offer?

Virtually every hotel/conference center today offers large and small meeting rooms, good sound and video projection services, and breakfast and other food services for attendees on conference days. But the fact that most venues offer those things doesn't mean they are all the same.

Here are some other features you should be looking for as you select a conference setting:

- **The most pleasant hotel location** you can afford. Locations near bodies of water, or with beautiful mountain views, can do a lot to enhance the quality of your convention experience.
- **Large, bright meeting rooms** with windows and good ventilation. If you have ever spent a few conference days stuck in a basement-level meeting room with no natural light, you know how exhausting it can be.

- **Convenient common areas** with Wi-Fi where attendees can spend time, make calls and check their messages and email between sessions.
- **Nearby access to food,** both within the hotel facility and, if possible, at other restaurants nearby. Conference attendees often find it pleasant and energizing to be able to go to local eateries with colleagues instead of spending time only in the conference venue.
- **Outdoor seating areas,** if the setting and season permit.

Special Experiences and Exclusive Outings

There are times when you want your employees to arrive, learn as much as you can teach them in a short period of time, and send them on their way back home. Sometimes, that is the kind of experience your employees would like too.

But if your venue is located in a beautiful setting, you might also consider planning some meaningful experiences for your attendees. Some possibilities include a harbor cruise, a trip to a nearby natural setting, or a meal in a famous restaurant that serves regional cuisine.

Again, the event planner at the hotel you are considering will be able to recommend the "best of the best" experiences for your group in the area and should also be able to negotiate discounted rates at local eateries and attractions.

Special Accommodations for Employees who Have Mobility and other Concerns

Modern conference centers today are well equipped to offer considerate and appropriate rooms and settings for any of your people who have mobility or other limitations. If you are considering holding your conference in an older or historical hotel, however, be sure to ask about this issue.

Tips for Choosing and Using the Best Trainers and Speakers

Are you inviting a professional trainers speaker to deliver your training at your off-site? Perhaps to offer you a motivational keynote that sets a buzz that will keep energy high?

If you are, you are making an investment that can make your event memorable, transformational . . . and maybe even sensational. But what steps should you take to assure that the speaker will be the right one, and that he or she will produce results that will exceed your expectations in every way?

Here are some great tips from Katrina Mitchell, CEO of Speak!

- **Determine** your date, time of session, location, budget and top three learning objectives for the session that you are considering a speaker for. A prospective speaker or a speakers' bureau will need these basic details before they can help you get started.
- **Identify** a theme and set goals and/or learning objectives for your conference and for each session you want an outside presenter to address. Setting learning objectives out of the gate will help your bureau and meeting planner partners find the best possible speaker "match" for you without wasting your time with options that are not a fit. An experienced bureau will

also deliver relevant options that fit your system, culture and your budget.

- **Understand** the different types of speakers and choose the one best suited to help you meet your objectives. Some speakers are better positioned as ROCK STAR opening keynoters, some are more TACTICAL, and some are fantastic CLOSERS.
- **Pick** the best speaker for the time slot. For example, after dinner is not the best time to program a high content speaker. Your employees will be more tuned in and able to retain a business message during the day. An evening spot is better suited for a short motivational message, entertainment or humor.
- **Start** with your end-result in mind. Ask yourself: "What do we want our people to think, feel, say or do when this session is over?"
- **Ask** whether your prospective speaker or bureau partner really understands your business. Listen carefully to the questions they are asking you.
- **Review** recommendations, watch preview videos and check references for the speaker before making your final selection. Once you feel you have a good candidate, get your team on a call with the potential speaker to be sure they are the right fit. If you are working with an experienced bureau partner, they will have vetted the speaker before the options were ever presented to you. "That's another reason to partner with a bureau!" Mitchell advises.

- **Remember** that just because someone may be an expert, that doesn't mean they have the platform skills to get what they know across and make the learning process fun and engaging. Look for the presenter's credentials and experience speaking in front of groups like yours. Though subject matter experts certainly have value, they can often miss the mark if they can't communicate effectively to your group.
- **Make sure** your speaker is an expert at customizing the program to hit a bullseye for you. Involve the speaker in your planning process so everyone is clear on the mission and vision of the event.
- **Include** any details regarding special room set up or AV needs, selling books or additional programs in your contract so there are no surprises at the last minute. A professional bureau will help you manage all these details up front and prevent any last-minute headaches from occurring.

Bonus Tip from Katrina Mitchell:

Think back! On your preliminary calls, did the speakers you contacted talk mostly about themselves, or were they genuinely interested in learning about your business and goals for the conference and the session? When a speaker starts out making it all about themselves, that typically doesn't change when they arrive on site.

Some Tips on Making Great Speaker Introductions

To set your speaker up for success from the moment they take the stage, the speaker intro is pivotal!

An effective speaker intro should:

- **Be short.**
- **Grab attention** and focus on why you chose the speaker to address your audience.
- **Provide credibility** for the speaker—so they do not need to spend valuable presentation time doing this themselves. Remember that when you say great things about your speaker, what you say is credible. If your speaker says wonderful things about him or herself, the intro can come off as arrogant and off-putting.
- **Let your audience know** a bit about why the speaker was chosen for them. For example, a powerful way to introduce your speaker to your audience is to start with just a few words (before the speaker's actual introduction) on why this particular speaker was carefully chosen to be there. This will help set up the speaker's qualifications and credibility and emphasize the care that was taken to find the perfect person to address your group. Let your audience know how much you care about them and the effort that went into bringing them an experience that will help them grow both personally and professionally!

Sample of a good introduction:

"After reviewing countless speakers to come and share their stories with you today, the convention committee finally settled on (Name of Speaker Here) and I can't tell you how excited we are. (Speaker First Name) was hands-down a perfect choice for us because of his unparalleled franchise experience, global recognition as a customer service expert, and personal success in running award-winning franchise units himself."

This advice will raise the quality and professionalism well above of the typical, predictable speaker intro!

How to Get the Most from Your Speaker Investment

Here are some tips from Katrina Mitchell of Speak!

- **Be vulnerable when helping your speaker plan.** Help your speaker understand what's really going on within your company —what are your challenges? What are your biggest triumphs? Dive into the current and future issues you are facing.
- **Fill out a Pre-Program Questionnaire.** Pre-Program Questionnaires help your speaker understand your culture, key terminology, and sensitive issues.
- **Connect your speaker to your employees in advance.** Give your speaker an opportunity to connect with a selection of your employees as one of their pre-program research resources.
- **Create energy before the session with pump-'em-up music!** Prior to and as attendees are entering the meeting room, have high-energy music playing that is relevant to your theme.
- **Create excitement and anticipation.** Open the doors at one time. Let everyone rush in at once, creating energy, rather than straggling in. *Bonus benefit:* This creates an opportunity for even more contact and networking for your group as they gather outside.
- **Don't allow your attendees to spread out throughout the room.** This is especially important if the room is set for a much larger number of guests than you expect.

- **Don't have your first row too far away from the stage.** A good speaker wants to create a connection and rapport with the audience—most suggest having the first row about six feet away from the stage.
- **Don't have extra chairs if you don't need them.** Stack extras in the back of the room, to be used if needed. The goal is to create an energetic "epicenter" in the room and not dilute it.
- **Rope off all the seats in the back of the room.** Create excitement around having your people sit up front by giving away prizes or hiding a prize under one of the chairs in the first three rows. Be creative!
- **Use your home office staff as energetic ushers and brand cheerleaders.** Have them line the aisles when the doors are opened, high-fiving, greeting your audience members by name – maybe even chanting your theme. Make it fun!
- **Introduce your speaker.** A short, punchy intro delivered with enthusiasm and energy allows your speaker to take the stage and dive straight into the story, grabbing your audience from the start.
- **Make sure you have a second microphone on the platform.** This may be used for a seamless speaker introduction, to allow the speaker to leave the stage to engage the audience or as a back-up if the primary mic malfunctions.
- **Have a sound and tech check before the talk begins.** This is critical. Beware of speakers who say they don't need an audio

check—perhaps they don't really care about ensuring a successful outcome.

- **Invest in stage lighting and kick it up a notch!** House lighting is often weak and hazy, especially in older venues. Often, it's not possible to see the speaker clearly from the back of the room.
- **Turn the lights UP!** Your speaker is watching the audience for reactions and will adapt his or her presentation on the fly, based on what he or she is seeing.
- **Keep the room cool.** Cooler temps keep attendees on their toes and engaged—and the speaker from sweating!
- **Set the temperature and leave it.** When adjusting temperature during a session, you're seeking a quick change! This often overcorrects and creates wild swings in temperature.
- **Tell attendees to bring layers.** By planning ahead, everyone can be comfortable with the temperature, regardless of personal preferences (which can vary greatly).
- **Clear space to move around the stage.** Most speakers are "walkers and talkers." An open stage gives them the freedom to move.
- **If a podium is necessary, position it six feet back from the front of the stage or away from the first row of seats, and to one side.** The ideal situation is to remove the podium, but we suggest this alternative when needed.
- **Position stage stairs in the center of your stage if possible.** A position in the center allows your speaker to quickly create an on-

the-spot interaction with your audience and get back on the stage in a seamless flow.

- **Make sure that everyone can clearly see the presenter.** Check for visual obstructions and if needed, adjust seating so that every seat has a clear line of sight to the speaker.
- **For any audience with more than 300 members, use large IMAG monitors that show your speaker.** The term IMAG is a short for "image magnification." An IMAG monitor allows audience members seated far from the stage to see details of the performer's body language and facial expressions.
- **Record your session for internal use post-event** (with speaker approval, of course). If you are using IMAG, your AV crew will be in place and ready to record.

Should You Use an Interpreter to Sign for the Hearing-Impaired?

Because it is costly to hire an interpreter who can sign for members of your audience who are hearing-impaired, we suggest polling your attendees before the conference to ask whether they need or would benefit from having one.

For help in finding a good interpreter, visit the online directory of them that is maintained by the Registry of Interpreters for the Deaf. You can also ask the event planner at your conference center venue to help you hire an interpreter that has been used at the same venue in the past.

Part Five: What's All This About Metrics?

Many company leaders think that measuring the results of their company training will give them information that is "nice to know."

If that is what you have been thinking, We would like to challenge you in this article. We would like to prove to you that measuring what is happening with your company training can empower you and improve your profits and processes in immense ways that will astound you.

A Case Study that Proves the Point

When Tortal Training was analyzing training activities for a restaurant chain, we looked at the profits of individual restaurants in two categories:

- Restaurants where 50% or less of employees were taking the required online training
- Restaurants where 80% or more of employees were taking the required online training

Our analysis showed that in the second group, the annual growth rate of business was 4% greater than the growth rate at restaurants in the first.

Since the average restaurant in the chain was doing an average of $2 million annually, that meant that restaurants where at least 80% of employees were taking training were doing $80,000 more in business every year. Even when we subtracted the $20,000 cost of the food that was being prepared and sold from that figure of $80,000, we determined that each training-invested location was still doing $60,000 more business every year than locations that were less invested in training. Of course growth compounds every year.

And in the restaurant chain we analyzed, there were 1,200 locations where 50% or fewer of the employees were completing the training. So that means that if each of those locations raised its training percentage to 80%, they had the opportunity to contribute an additional $96 million to franchise-wide sales. That is an astounding result of simply getting more employees to take training that was already available. Put in dollar terms, the franchisor lost $5.7 million in royalties and close to $2 million in national fund dollars. The franchisees in total lost $69 million after food cost and franchise fees.

So our question to you is, would you be willing to leave $96 million on the table every year, just by failing to get at least 80% of all employees to take the training you have already paid to develop and are already providing? Or if you don't have great training, what would you be willing to invest to improve sales by 4%?

Let's Review . . .

It is worth finding out the impact of those that truly use your training vs. those that don't, to find out what you're leaving on the table.

Of course, you may be thinking you don't have great online training or any training. If that is the case, what would you be willing to invest to improve sales by 4%?

Three major take-aways from this example are:

1. You should know what the impact of your training is
2. You should look at training as an investment, not a cost
3. Your franchisees need to realize that training is an investment with a high return

Those figures offer a compelling argument for training. But perhaps more importantly, they document the importance of developing and measuring metrics to understand what is taking place in your training efforts. In this case, we simply compared growth rates in locations where high percentages of employees were taking training against what was taking place in locations where low percentages of employees were taking part.

But you have to ask the right questions to uncover the wisdom that statistics can teach – questions that are both imaginative and curious. In the case study we have just discussed, wisdom was unlocked when we decided to ask, "Are profits stronger in locations where more people are taking the training and if they are, what kind of statistics apply?" With imagination, you can develop similar questions to explore through data. If customer satisfaction levels are higher at some of your locations, for example, what percentage of the employees there are taking and completing training? If customer satisfaction is low at other locations, are there certain courses that employees have *not* completed?

Curiosity might have killed the cat, but it never contributed to poor company performance. Ask a lot of curious questions and learn.

Build Soft Metrics into Your Training Development

Because the first aim of training is to improve the way people do things, all training programs measure hard metrics like these after training is done:

- Are our salespeople making **more sales calls, closing more sales**, or increasing the **size of the average order?**
- Have our product assemblers **increased their output** and **reduced the number of quality defects?**
- Are our phone reps now resolving **more customer issues** on the first call?
- How many more **positive reviews** are we getting online?
- Six months after training ends, are more customers **placing repeat orders**?

Without metrics like those, how will you know whether your training has achieved its goals or repaid your investment?

What About Soft Metrics?

Soft metrics have to do less with observable performance, and more to do with attitudes. They too are measured before and after training as a way to evaluate results. Some examples:

- Do members of your hotel's front desk staff **feel calmer and more confident** about resolving customer complaints?

- Do your new hires now feel **more enthusiastic about working for your company** than they did before training began?
- Do employees now expect to **remain at your company** for longer periods of time?
- Has training improved **employees' attitudes**?

Soft metrics can help predict how "sticky" your training will be. For example, employees who feel dramatically more committed to your company will be less likely to fall back into old patterns in the months after training ends.

Another reason to measure soft metrics is that they help you identify any extra benefits your training achieved. The primary purpose of your training was to teach your restaurant workers to deliver better customer service, for example, but they also became bigger believers in your brand.

The Art of Measuring Soft Metrics

There is an incorrect assumption that it is difficult to collect data on soft metrics. In fact, soft metrics can be measured by having trainees complete surveys or have interviews with members of your training or HR team.

Another way to gauge soft metrics is to measure behaviors. After training your call center staffers, for example, do they arrive more punctually and call in sick less often? That could indicate improved motivation and morale. Or after training your retail salespeople, has the rate of their retention improved after six months or a year? That could indicate that your training made their jobs less stressful and more satisfying.

Evaluating Hard and Soft Metrics Yields a Fuller Picture or Results

When evaluating training success, it is not a question of measuring hard metrics *versus* soft metrics. Why not measure both? Think of them as different tiles in a larger mosaic that yields a picture of everything your training is accomplishing.

How to Measure whether Your Learners Are Using their New Skills after Training Ends

It is not always necessary to create entirely new training programs to achieve the results you want. Instead, you can ask. . .

Are your trainees really using the new skills they learned in training?

Here are seven strategies that can help assure that they are:

1. **During training, explain what you will be measuring later on.** This sounds basic, but it can be effective. For example, if one of your goals is to have your salespeople follow up a minimum of four times before giving up on a sale, tell them they will be tracked on that. There is wisdom in the old saying, "What gets measured, gets done."
2. **Schedule additional training sessions.** This sounds pretty fundamental too, yet some companies seem to assume that once training is done, it's done. The fact is, follow-up sessions can be highly effective in making sure that training "sticks." To reduce costs, you can deliver follow-up content in online lessons or to mobile devices.
3. **Let trainees monitor and support each other.** Try setting up weekly calls where trainees check in with each other to ask, "What have you tried so far . . . how is it working for you?" This can be more effective than having upper management look in.

4. **Follow training with coaching.** Your trainer can take on a coaching role and work directly with trainees after training ends. Or executives within your organization can.
5. **Use technology to keep things percolating.** You can send a daily tip or motivational message or video to trainees via text messages or email. Tortal Training can help you integrate them seamlessly into your training program at very little cost.
6. **Shake up the way your trainees do their jobs.** Instead of having each member of your sales staff make sales calls alone, for example, let them partner up and make sales calls in pairs. It can be a great way to make sure your trainees step out of their comfort zones and try new things.
7. **Consider adding incentives or awards.** When a customer service rep successfully hits one of the benchmarks you set out in training, you can give her an award and share that news with all the other trainees. Used in the right way, awards can assure that more of your learners apply the lessons they learned in training.

Because we live in modern times, there is a simple answer to that question . . .

Use a modern Learning Management System (LMS) to gather data

A full-featured LMS makes statistics like these instantly available to you:

- How many of your employees in each location have **started** training programs? How many of them have **completed** training?
- How many employees do you have who are taking training, how many of them have **completed certification programs,** and which of those employees are contributing most to sales and profits?
- Which of your training programs are causing the greatest levels of improvement in **employee performance,** which can be measured by online customer reviews, repeat business, and other metrics?
- A good LMS will measure what percentage of employees in every location are taking **live training,** onboarding, mentoring, etc. Are you tracking these numbers?
- Which of your training programs are **increasing profits** in locations where they have been used . . . and which are not?

As you develop questions you can explore using your LMS, remember there are many economic and other factors that training can impact upon, including:

- **Sales,** including average sale size, closing rates and repeat business
- **Customer satisfaction,** as evaluated by your Net Promoter Score or other measures.
- **Brand awareness** among customers served.
- **Measurable improvements in safety** achieved after training that have resulted in lower insurance costs.
- **Employee** retention Improvements.

If you measure factors like those before and after training, you can gain a deeper understanding of the impact that training is having on your profits and operations.

We all know that training pays. But as the case study I shared at the beginning of this article shows, using metrics the right way empowers you to deploy your training efforts where they will produce the greatest results.

There is no mistake about it . . . training pays! But you will never know how much until you measure!

"If you aren't measuring it, it probably isn't happening."
- **Evan Hackel, CEO, Tortal Training**

Evan is right. If you're not measuring what your training is getting done, chances are nothing is changing.

That means that if you are not using metrics, you have probably agreed to live with the following problems:

- **You are spending money** but have no way to understand what you are getting in return.
- **You don't know** what you have accomplished with your training and, even worse, you have no way to improve your training efforts in the future.
- **Some of your employees** are doing a great job, some are doing a poor job, but you really don't know who they are, because you are not measuring what they do.
- **Your trainees are bored** and perplexed, because your training is teaching them all kinds of skills they don't really need – and failing to teach them the skills they need.
- **Your company's profits** and competitive edge are suffering, because you are not fixing critical problems that need your attention.
- **You're probably not doing a good job** of onboarding new employees, because you don't know what you should be teaching them or how to measure it.

We could continue to list problems that affect companies that fail to measure the effectiveness of their training. But let's do something more useful, by providing a quick overview of what metrics are.

The Process

You might want to print out this list and post it over your desk where you can see it every day. It will help you develop training that brings about the change you need in your organization . . .

1. **Identify the processes** that you would like your training to improve.
2. **Pinpoint** key indicators you can measure to understand whether your training is bringing about the changes you want in those processes.
3. **Create and deliver training** that focuses on the processes you are trying to improve.
4. **Monitor** your key indicators after training to determine whether performance has improved.

If you follow those steps, you will have a way to evaluate the overall success of your training efforts.

Here's an example of how one company used that structure to create high-ROI training that brought about meaningful change in the way employees were performing a critical job.

Improving the Skills of Appliance Installers

A chain of appliance stores had a capable group of deliverer/installers who were doing a good job. They delivered and installed washers, dryers, refrigerators and other appliances. They never damaged customers' property or made installation mistakes that required them to visit customers a second time. Yet in surveys that were given to customers after their appliances had been installed, customers were giving an average of only three stars out of five to the installers. What was going wrong?

When company management dug into the issue, they discovered that two product installers were consistently earning five-star reviews from customers after they had delivered and installed appliances. What were these two employees doing that was different from what other installers were doing?

The company spent time with them and asked them to describe, step-by-step, their process of delivering and installing appliances. After interviewing those two employees, the company determined that they were doing several things that other installers were not

- **Appliance installer one** was taking the owner's manual out of its poly bag and was sitting down with customers (usually at their kitchen table) to go through the manual, explain how to use the appliance, and answer questions.
- **Appliance installer two** was starting dishwashers and clothes washers, usually with customers present, to make sure that there were no problems and that customers understood how to use their new appliances.
- **Both installers asked,** "Do you have any questions or concerns?" before they left customers' homes.
- **Appliance installer two** also gave customers a business card before he left and said, "Call me today if you have any issues."

The company decided that it had the opportunity to improve customer satisfaction by training all installers to make those same steps part of every appliance installation. So it added a new unit to its training program that taught those skills.

How would the company measure improvements in customer satisfaction after the training? Luckily, it already had data from previous satisfaction surveys that customers had completed.

So the company identified, and started to measure, these metrics:

- **Would the new training result** in an average satisfaction rating of 4.5+ stars on customer satisfaction surveys after appliances were installed, which would represent an improvement from the current average rating of 4?
- **Would the comments** that customers wrote in on their surveys become at least 50% more positive? A statistical analysis of past surveys indicated that about one in 10 surveys contained a negative comment. Post-training, could that number be cut at least in half?

How would the company measure improvements in customer satisfaction after the training? Luckily, it already had data from previous satisfaction surveys that customers had completed.

So the company identified, and started to measure, these metrics:

- **Would the new training result** in an average satisfaction rating of 4.5+ stars on customer satisfaction surveys after appliances were installed, which would represent an improvement from the current average rating of 4?

- **Would the comments** that customers wrote in on their surveys become at least 50% more positive? A statistical analysis of past surveys indicated that about one in 10 surveys contained a negative comment. Post-training, could that number be cut at least in half?

The company's new training, which was tightly focused on changing only four of the steps installers were following, hit those targets within only four months. And even better, the company noticed that other measurables were improving too. Repeat business was increasing, for example, and the quality of the company's online reviews improved.

Part Six: Modern Features that Make for Great Training

Training on Smartphones: Six Critical Questions to Ask Before You Begin

You look around your company one day and notice that most of your employees seem to be glued to their smartphones. When they're not working, they're shopping, accessing social media, texting with friends, watching videos, reading the news . . . you name it. Your eyes aren't fooling you. According to the best statistics we have been able to find, in some companies more than 80% of employees have smartphones.

Another Set of Statistics to Think About

With all those smartphone users all around your company, it only makes sense to jump right in and start delivering your training to mobile devices, right? Well maybe yes, maybe no.

If you spend some time reading "U.S. Smartphone Use in 2015," a far-ranging new report about smartphone usage from the Pew Research Center, you'll find some statistics that are a little troubling. Although smartphone use has increased dramatically (in 2011, only 35% of adult Americans owned them; today, 64% do), 48% of "smartphone-dependent" Americans have experienced service interruptions because they were unable to keep up with their payments. And who are the most "smartphone-dependent" Americans? According to the Pew research, many of them are younger Americans – possibly the same group of people you are trying to reach with your training?

So you need to ask questions before you jump on the mobile training bandwagon. Here are some we think you should ask before you call your training development company to say, "It's time to put our training on phones."

Question One: How long will our training program be around?

If you're creating a program that you project will be used for several years or longer, then it could make sense to spend money to create training that will be delivered via smartphones. If you are launching a program that you will only use for months or weeks, more traditional delivery options (like online programs, videos or classroom instruction) could better serve your needs and cost a lot less to launch.

Question Two: How often will our mobile training materials need to be updated, and what will that cost?

Remember that training materials often need to be updated to reflect new products, new processes, marketplace trends and other factors. Sometimes training materials simply need to be improved. Remember to ask your training development company how much it will cost to revise your mobile-delivered materials in the future. Unless you ask ahead of time and get an agreement in writing, you could end up with a mobile training program that will cost too much to maintain.

Question Three: What phones do my trainees use and how do they use them?

Chances are good that many, if not most, of your trainees are using current iPhones and Android devices. But it is smart to find out before you develop a mobile program. Several considerations come into play. First, if 10% or 15% of your trainees have devices that will prevent them from accessing your training, is that acceptable? Second, what will it cost to develop training materials that will work across a range of devices that could now include Apple, Android, BlackBerry and even Google phones? Talk to your training development company early in the planning process to get a bead on costs.

Question Four: Am I only thinking of adapting our current training materials to run on mobile devices?

As a training professional, you already know that it is unrealistic to expect your current web-based training programs to display and function correctly on smartphones. The fact is that delivering your current training programs on smartphones can work best if you start with a clean sheet of paper and create all-new materials from the ground up. We urge you to discuss that issue with your training development company.

Question Five: How should mobile delivery influence training planning and design?

This is a very big question that you should tackle in-depth with your training director or consultant. Here are some considerations that come into play . . .

- **Lesson length and curriculum design**. Lessons that seem to be just the right length when delivered on computer terminals generally seem too long on phones. So don't be surprised if you have to double the number of lessons to cover the same material.
- **Video integration.** Videos need to be chosen and formatted to provide an engaging viewer experience on mobile devices.
- **Interactive features.** Response forms and questionnaires that work just right on a laptop or tablet screen might not function on smartphones' smaller screens.
- **Uniform performance across platforms.** Training materials must be created not only to function well, but to work perfectly on iPhones, Androids, Blackberries and the rest.

Question Six: Should we develop a company training app?

In many cases, the answer to this question is yes. As long as you are developing online training programs, a convenient app can encourage more of your learners to log in, use your training, and make it part of their routine.

But tread carefully and talk to your training development company before you jump on board and agree to create a proprietary company training app. One reason is that an app is never just one app, but several that function on different mobile devices. Further, an app needs to be updated and maintained as you launch future training programs.

All that can add to your development costs more quickly than you expect.

"Don't Be Lazy with Social Learning," a post that Chris Browning wrote for the ATD Learning Technologies Blog on April 6th, makes some excellent points about why social media channels can be ineffective for learning purposes. To quote from his post . . .

> *"If I see a three-minute video or read a blog that I like, I can quickly share it with my network, with the thought that they too might enjoy it and learn something new. Some folks in my network may even reply with a `thanks for sharing,' or `interesting read.' So what's wrong with that? Nothing, per se. It's just lazy to assume that simply allowing people to share and comment is sufficient."*

Chris Browning is making the point that liking or forwarding material to other people does not usually allow them to absorb information fully. As he points out, genuine social learning is actually *social* – a learning experience that takes place when people convene face-to-face to share information and experiences, ask questions, and do things together. The insights that people learn directly from each other tend to be better absorbed and longer remembered than lessons that they only read about.

Where Genuine Social Learning Can Take Place during Training

Although he surely knows them, Chris Browning doesn't write in his post about some of the ways genuine social learning can enhance training. Here are some uses that we at Tortal have seen work effectively:

- **Simulated or actual projects** that let small groups of people solve a problem or – often better – work together on an actual project in the weeks or months after the formal training ends. That kind of social, experiential learning promotes change and "sticks."
- **Break-out discussions** in which a room full of trainees form smaller groups to discuss an issue, find a solution, or develop questions to ask when the whole room comes together again.
- **Games,** in which trainees interact with each other to solve a problem and learn lessons from each other as a result. Some people think that long-lasting, important lessons can't be taught through games. If you have ever seen how well games can work, you will see those people are wrong.

The Benefits of Custom eLearning Solutions for Corporate Training

If your company needs to train a defined group of employees who perform a specific function – retail salespeople, automotive service writers, front-desk hotel employees, food handlers – it is tempting to hire a training company that has a program that is ready to go. You call the company, find out what the training costs, set up a room and let that training company deliver its course to your employees.

That approach has its advantages. You don't have to invest your staff's time to develop specialized training. You don't have to hire training designers. You just unlock the door to your training room and let it all happen.

The problem is that after the training is done, you could discover that it failed to meet your needs, for reasons like these:

- It taught skills that your employees **really don't use or need.**
- Conversely, it **failed to teach specific skills** that your employees actually do need.
- The trainer the company sent had **no personal experience** doing the kind of work your employees do. Your trainees therefore didn't feel they could learn anything from him or her.
- Now that the training is finished, you have **no way to deliver it again** to more employees without hiring the training company again.

- You were only able to train employees in **one location.** To present the same training to employees who work in your field offices or other regions, you will have to hire the training company again.
- You have **no way to measure** the results of the training. You just sit back and hope that your employees learned something and that their performance improved.
- The training did nothing to **promote an understanding of your <u>brand,</u>** because it was generic. Today, it could be that other employees at another company down the street are getting the same training your company's trainees received last week.

Customized Training Is the Solution

Of course you already knew that. But chances are you don't want to think about creating customized training because it will be too expensive.

To do it, you assume you will have to create a training department and staff it up with expert training developers. After you hire them, they won't have enough work to do, because you only need to design training programs infrequently. So you think that despite the shortcomings of hiring that training company you used last time, you reach for the phone and hire them again. It is the simplest approach.

But there is another solution. You can hire a training development company that has proven expertise in developing customized training programs. Will that be too expensive? Of course, that is a question you need to ask. But instead of operating from a position of fear about the cost, you can start discussions from a strong position. You can decide what your budget for your training is, tell the training development company "This is what we have to spend," and see what they can do.

In many cases, you will get much more "bang for the buck" than you expected. A training development company that wants your business will be motivated to deliver you as much value as possible. It wants to win your business and show you what it can do. That means you have leverage, and that you will probably get a much bigger ROI on your training dollars than you were anticipating, and more full-featured training than you would have gotten if you simply reached for the phone.

Why Customized Training Delivers a Much Greater ROI

Here are some of the reasons why . . .

- **You teach employees the skills they actually need,** because your training development company starts by closely analyzing what your employees do and what they *need to do* to perform their jobs.
- **You get content that reinforces your brand,** because it has been created specifically for you. It incorporates your logo, shows your employees and customers, and tells your company story to your trainees.
- **Your training can include games,** videos, quizzes and other engaging content that

makes it "stickier" and more effective than simply having a presenter go before your group to talk.

- **Your training has trackable results,** because it will be integrated with your company's Learning Management System (LMS). You will know how many employees are taking your training, how many have completed it, how they have performed on exams that were embedded in your training, and more. And thanks to the LMS, you will be able to reinforce training concepts after the training is finished by sending your employees reminders to use what they learned, by sending out new training prompts, and more.

- **You can measure the results of your training,** because you and your training development company built training around metrics. Instead of just opening the door of your training room and hoping something changes, you can measure the improvements that your training achieved. Did it teach your retail salespeople to increase the size of their average sale, for example? Did it reduce errors on your production line? Did it motivate your food servers to deliver the kind of customer experience that resulted in a 50% improvement in your customers' satisfaction in surveys they fill out? The ability to measure means that you know what your training has achieved. That's critical. You wouldn't buy a new phone system for your company, or a new heating system, without having any idea what you are paying for. Why are you thinking about doing that with your training?

Plus, Customized Training Can Grow with You

Customized training that your employees complete on cellphones and tablets can be one of the most effective ways to deliver cost-effective training that yields a high ROI for your training dollars.

There are questions to consider before you take this route to delivering your training. How many of your employees have smartphones, for example? If some of your employees don't have them, what will it cost to buy enough tablets for them to use when taking their training? Is there excellent Wi-Fi connectivity in the company locations where you want them to train?

You and your training development company need to ask questions like those before you commit to developing training that will be delivered to trainees on tablets or phones. But after considering those issues, you will probably decide to consider mobile training even more seriously. It provides benefits like these:

- **You can train employees who work in all your locations** without incurring additional expense.
- **When your company expands and adds new employees,** your training program can be delivered to them repeatedly, without developing new training or spending more money.

- **You can revise your existing training programs rapidly** and economically, because they are "in your system." When you need to teach your employees additional new skills, there is no need to build new training programs from the ground up.
- **You can gain the ability to connect and communicate** with your employees on their smartphones. You can send out reminders about what they learned in training, announce the availability of new training, and more. Enhanced communication capabilities like those are another high-value benefit that mobile training offers, at very little extra expense.

How to Keep Training Development Costs Under Control

One of the most effective ways to increase the ROI on your training is to spend less on it. That might sound like we are making a joke, but we are not. Boosting you ROI isn't about spending more and getting more in return. It is about spending a reasonable amount and getting returns that far exceed your expectations.

How can you do that? Let us conclude this article with some actionable recommendations:

- **Decide on a budget** before you contact a training development company like Tortal Training. See what you can get for what you have to spend. A good training development company will work with you, make recommendations, and help you maximize your ROI.

- **Have an idea** of exactly what you want your training to achieve, and how you will measure results. Your training development company should help you in this process, by interviewing your current employees, analyzing the systems they use, pinpointing areas that can be improved, and more.

- **Ask about customizable content** that could be right for your training needs. Tortal, for example, offers Out of the Box Training Solutions that can be customized to help you reach your training objectives while controlling costs at the same time.

- **Don't forget** to think about the future. Yes, your training development company is helping you to design the training that you need right now. But to get much more value from working with that company, think about the future too. If you are about to expand company operations to a different state, talk about that. If you are planning to introduce a new line of products next year, don't forget to mention that. The more you can anticipate your future training needs as you develop the training you need right now, the more cost-effective your training will be.

Why Companies that Train Need to Know about SCORM

If you use computerized training materials of any kind, you need to understand what SCORM is and what it can do for you. In five minutes or fewer, this chapter will explain what you need to know.

SCORM, which stands for "Sharable Content Object Reference Model," was created back in 1999 when the U.S. Department of Defense saw a need for a standardized format for computerized learning materials. One year later, the Department of Defense launched its first version of SCORM, SCORM 1.0. In the years since, more versions have been released.

The Overview

SCORM is a standardized format for computerized materials. When videos, audio files, text, PowerPoints, interactive tests, and other content have been converted to SCORM format, they all work together seamlessly. Furthermore, the fact that they are all SCORM-compliant means that a learning designer can assemble and edit a training course in a more efficient and straightforward way. That's because the whole course, no matter what it contains, has been converted to one piece of editable computer code.

What Does SCORM Look Like? (The Tech Stuff)

When you convert all kinds of files – text files, PowerPoint presentations, videos, audio files, PDFs, and just about anything else - to be SCORM compliant, what really happens is that you are converting them into strings of HTML that you can insert into your master course.

That's the tech stuff. But how do you generate that HTML? You can be a computer programmer. There are also plenty of apps and software programs that can convert all kinds of files to SCORM. Or you can rely on an experienced training development company like Tortal to do the conversions and make sure that everything works just right on your company LMS.

Why Has SCORM Become the Standard?

In the years since SCORM was launched, it has been widely adopted by companies that create or use computerized training. Why has SCORM become the standard? Because it delivered benefits like these . . .

Older training materials – everything from printed handbooks to old videos – can be updated, converted to SCORM, and used in new training.

All training courses can be easily uploaded into a company's Learning Management System (LMS), because they are SCORM-compliant.

When new courses are created, they will run just like the other courses in an LMS, because they are also SCORM compliant.

New videos, quizzes and other training materials can be written and integrated into existing training courses, because they are SCORM compliant. So training content becomes editable.

This Story Illustrates the Need for SCORM

Here's an analogy. Let's say that instead of trying to create a training course, you are trying to create a video that you want to show at your grandmother's 80th birthday party. The good news is, you have a lot of materials that you can use in the video. The problem is, they are in different formats. You have photographs on paper, JPEGs on your computer, old home movies that are on reel-to-reel film, old videos on your computer, old audio files that are on cassettes, and more.

If all those materials were in the same format, putting together your video would be a snap. But because they aren't, you have to first get all those materials into certain compatible formats so you can merge them together into a video.

SCORM-compliant content works in much the same way. If you are creating a new training course and all your materials have been converted to SCORM, assembling them into one training course becomes a simple, drag and drop process. The result? You save time and money when you create training courses, they run correctly on your company's LMS, and you can expand and edit them in the future.

How to Create Training Content that Conforms to the SCORM Standard

One way is to poke around online, find (and probably purchase) a product that will convert your old PowerPoints and other materials to SCORM, and give it a try. Some of these programs also have authoring capabilities, meaning that you can use them to create training courses with all-new content. Experience has shown that these conversion apps can convert certain files, like PowerPoints, but that it can be difficult and time-consuming to create a full-featured course that embodies the videos, audios, quizzes and other features that you want in your training program. Plus, most of those programs require you to use templates when creating training courses. That's easy, but the result is that the courses you create can end up looking generic.

A second way is to hire a training development company like Tortal Training. We have been creating SCORM-compliant training for years, which assures that all your training content will perform correctly, according to the following standards . . .

Course materials, even older videos and other files that were created years ago, will be converted to new SCORM-compliant formats and will play and perform perfectly.

New SCORM-compliant courses can be written, uploaded to your company's LMS, and go live.

Courses can be edited and updated easily, and they will perform perfectly in your LMS and be trackable.

A third way is to use Tortal Training's Course Authoring Tool, which is available at no additional cost to all Tortal Training clients who are using Tortal's Learning Management System (LMS). The Course Authoring Tool lets you write new SCORM-compliant course materials, update older course materials, convert older Flash-based videos to newer formats, and do much more.

So, which approach is the best way to create SCORM-compliant course materials that you can update, integrate into your LMS, and more? It is up to you. Contact a Tortal Learning expert today to learn more.

A Quick Case Study

Tortal Training has developed and updated training programs for hundreds of clients This client's story illustrates the importance of SCORM.

"We need to create a new training program," that client told us, "but by the way, we don't want to toss our old training materials, we want to make them part of our new training."

That kind of request is not unusual. But the following things needed to happen . . .

An old printed employee handbook needed to be input, updated, and displayed in new and engaging ways to trainees.

Three old Flash-based videos about the company needed to be updated and converted to run in the new training program.

Older on-paper quizzes and tests needed to be input and converted to run on computers and mobile devices.

All training content had to integrate with the company's Tortal Learning Management System

(LMS) so that all employees' training use could be tracked.

All those goals were reached. How? By writing new material and reformatting old material to be SCORM-compliant.

The result, like that video that that man created for his grandmother's birthday, turned out to be a thing of beauty that performed perfectly. And in the case of the training, the beauty happened for only one reason . . .

All the content was SCORM-compliant

Part Seven: Why Your Company Needs Customer Service Training

Why You Need to Train Your People to Offer Your Customers a Great Experience

Can you think of a company that doesn't have any clients or customers? Frankly, we can't.

When we asked an executive we know to name a company that didn't have any clients or customers, he thought about it for a few minutes and then said, "A company that uses robots to dig mines on Mars, and that never has to deal directly with customers, might not have to think about customer service."

That was a good try. But even a company that sent mining robots to Mars would still need customers in order to survive. If the company is in the mining business, it needs to sell what it is pulling from beneath the surface of Mars to someone. And to make those sales, the company needs customers . . . and those customers need to be served.

Can't You Simply Hire People who are "Good with People" and Turn Them Loose?

You might also think that if you hire pleasant employees who have positive attitudes, customer service will pretty much take care of itself. Again, that is not an unintelligent assumption to make. The problem is that pleasing customers demands more of your employees than simply being pleasant. Successful results depend on specific skills.

What Customer Service Training Can Do for Your Organization

And to please your customers, you need to provide focused training that you design and deliver to achieve specific, results like these:

- **Increasing the size of an average sale.** Employees who know how to please customers simply sell more. Good customer service skills, if applied consistently, boost profits dramatically.
- **Increasing customer loyalty and repeat business.** No matter what kind of business you are in, you want repeat customers. And you get repeat customers because your employees have excellent customer service skills. If you are in the hospitality business, for example, you want the members of your hotel staff to provide the kind of excellent service that gets your guests to become loyal, repeat customers. Hitting that goal means defining specific skills that hotel personnel need to need to build repeat business. As with any other kind of training, you need to identify specific skills that can be taught or improved and develop training that addresses them.
- **Preventing and resolving conflict with customers and clients**. Carefully define the skills that your employees in all job roles need to resolve conflicts, answer questions, and please customers.
- **Anticipating and dealing with safety concerns.** You need employees who are trained to keep customers safe inside your facilities and in outdoor areas. You need employees who know how to respond to specific emergencies. Again, you need to

pinpoint specific skills and to train your
employees to practice them.

In summary . . .

Great customer service doesn't just "happen" —
even if you hire excellent people. It is something
you build and cultivate through training.

Critical Customer Service Aptitudes that Can Be
Trained

Let's assume that you have made the decision to
train certain groups of your employees to improve
their customer-service skills. For the purposes of
this chapter, let's also assume that you have
identified specific jobs and positions where your
employees interact with clients and customers, and
that you have decided to direct your training
efforts toward them.

Very good. You are on your way toward developing
and delivering training that can dramatically
improve the satisfaction levels experienced by your
clients and customers. But the next question is,
what specific skills and aptitudes do you need to
teach?

To answer that question, your first step is to
identify specific skills and activities that impact
most strongly on customer satisfaction. You can
pinpoint those skills by speaking with individuals
who fall into these groups . . .

- **The people who are currently performing
  the customer service jobs where you will
  direct your training efforts.** Which of their
  activities do they feel need improvement?
  Where do they feel they need to increase
  their knowledge? Where do they feel they
  lack the resources to perform their jobs
  successfully? Talk with them, listen to what
  they have to say, and create a list of

important skills to be improved through your training.

- **The managers who supervise your front-line employees.** From the perspective of these managers, are there recurring situations or problems that could be improved through training? If so, what specific activities are they, and what specific skills and aptitudes need to be addressed?
- **Customers and clients.** Survey them. Be sure to ask for suggestions about improving the quality of service you provide, about how problems they encountered could have been handled better, and more. If you have a list of customers who were displeased with something about the customer service they received from you, be sure to call them up and learn more about specific aspects of your customer service that should be improved.

Four Critical Areas to Focus Your Customer Service Training Efforts

As you talk to the people we listed just above – your employees, managers and your customers too – chances are you will discover that you can produce the most dramatic changes in your company's customer service by developing training in the following four areas.

Critical Customer Service Skill to Train: Systems

When customers are displeased with the level of service and attention they have received from a company, the underlying cause is often this . . .

The employee who was serving them was not completely trained to use company systems.

There are many instances when customers receive poor service for this reason, including these:

- **The customer wants to return a product,** but an employee does not know how to expedite the return.
- **A salesperson does not completely understand** how to use cash registers and other equipment.
- **A phone representative** in a customer service center doesn't know how to obtain authorization from a system that processes returns.

The fact is that when employees are trained to use your company equipment and systems, you prevent many customer service problems from arising in the first place. And the good news is, developing training to teach the needed skills is usually a simple and straightforward process.

Critical Customer Service Skill to Train: Listening Skills

Your customers can immediately sense whether or not your employees are really focusing on what they are saying. And if those clients sense that they are not being heard, they quickly become frustrated and dissatisfied with the quality of care you have provided.

Some of the critical listening skills to teach include:

- **The ability to completely focus** on what a customer is saying, while shutting out everything else that is taking place in the work area.
- **The skill to "read between the lines"** and identify the underlying solution that the customer is really talking about.
- **The skill to listen** for what the customer is saying that is valid and correct . . . and not what is wrong or inaccurate. When your employees can focus in that way and discuss what is valid in what the customer is saying, problems and issues can be resolved more quickly and satisfactorily.

Critical Customer Service Skill to Train: Conflict Resolution

Customers become more satisfied increase when they are dealing with employees who have been trained to resolve conflicts or – even better – to provide customers with solutions that prevent real conflict from arising at all.

Some skills that can be trained include:

- **Good listening, as we explained just above.** When customers know and sense that their concerns have been heard and understood, they understand that they are not in conflict with your organization. They are working with you to decide on a mutually positive and acceptable solution to the issue that is under discussion.
- **The ability to envision and suggest multiple solutions for an issue that is**

under discussion. When your employees are trained to identify and suggest a range of choices that will resolve an issue or remove an obstacle, levels of customer satisfaction soar.

- **The skills to implement a solution quickly, predictably and effectively.** Customers don't want to hear that you have worked with them to develop a theoretical solution to a concern they have. They are entitled to hear specifics. For example, their refund will be *immediately* credited to their bank account. Or they will meet with one of your bank officers in 30 minutes to discuss your mortgage refining options. The ability to plan and implement solutions is something that can be effectively trained.

Critical Customer Service Skill to Train: Autonomy and Decision-Making

Unfortunately, many of us have become accustomed to hearing frustrating statements like these when we are trying to resolve issues with companies we are going business with:

- "I am not authorized to approve your return."
- "Let me bring my manager in on this call."
- "I know you would like to send your product back to us, but first I have to get somebody to approve the return . . . can I put you on hold for five minutes?"

Instead, you can train your employees to use strategies like these that can dramatically improve the level of your customers' satisfaction:

- **Apply the "common sense rule"** that means that if a solution to a customer-related issue makes sense, they should go ahead and use it.
- **Exercise autonomy,** which means that they have the leeway to make independent decisions (within predetermined parameters) without asking their supervisors.

In Summary . . .

Simple, goal-centered training can go a long way toward assuring that your employees are delivering the kind of satisfying experiences and outcomes that your customers want and expect. Should you direct your attention to developing training in the critical area of customer satisfaction?

Yes, you should! The immediate improvement you see in repeat business and profits will surprise you.

What Kind of Training Works Best to Teach Customer Service Skills?

Many companies that would like to improve the customer service skills of their workforce hire motivational speakers who come in and deliver energizing and inspiring talks to employees.

There is a place for that. But in our experience, one-size-fits-all motivational sessions do not deliver meaningful, long-term improvements in the quality of customer service that a company's employees are able to deliver.

The place to start is to focus on the positions where improvements are needed – perhaps in your front-desk service writers in your muffler shop, in the beverage servers who work at your summer seaside resort, or in your employees who provide landscaping services for your customers. Once you have defined the jobs where you would like the quality of customer service to improve, your next two steps are to:

- **Define the specific tasks** or skills that need improvement.
- **Identify the metrics you will measure** before and after training to understand the effectiveness of the training you have provided.

Those are your starting considerations.

The good news about customer service training is that you can deliver it to your employees in a number of different ways. You can design live programs with live trainers and teach the needed skills that way. You can also design programs that you can have employees take on computers in your company training center or on their smartphones. Customer service skills can be effectively taught on computers, smartphones, and tablets. And once you have developed training programs to be delivered in that way, you can continue to roll out the same training programs to new trainees in the future. There is no need to develop new programs for every training class or new need, and that saves you money and increases the reach of your training.

Videos, Simulations and More

But what kind of learning experiences should your training include? Here are some that have been shown to work very well to teach customer service concepts and skills:

- **Interactive computerized games** that simulate situations that employees will deal with and solve on their jobs.
- **Simulations** that let trainees solve common customer service "issues" and conflicts.
- **Videos** that show common customer service challenges and explore solutions to them.
- **Interactive, live playacting scenarios** that let trainees pair off and explore possible solutions to problems.
- **Quizzes, tests** and other scored exercises that help you track your trainees' learning and progress.

Part Eight: How to Get the Most Value from Your Learning Management System

Have you decided that it is time to start using a Learning Management System (LMS) to organize and monitor your company's training activities?

If you have made that decision, congratulations. You have made a wise choice about taking your company training to the next level. But may we ask you a question . . .

Why did you decide that you needed an LMS?

Please stop and think about that question. Perhaps you decided that you need an LMS for one of the following reasons?

- You were having a difficult time **keeping track** of which of your employees were registered for your training program and participating. (This is a common motivation for starting to use an LMS.)
- You were unable to keep track of which of your employees had **completed** your training programs.
- Quizzes and tests are embedded in your training materials, but **you had no record** of how well your employees were performing on them.
- You had identified metrics that you would use to measure the results of your training. But without clear records of who was taking and completing your training, you had no way to **understand whether your training was resulting in improved performance**. (If

175

you don't know who to measure or what they learned, how can metrics be of any use?)

Keep Your Main Motivation in Mind . . .

Once you pinpoint your main motivation for turning to an LMS, write it down and don't forget it. Keep it top of mind as you select and work with an LMS provider as you ask the rest of the questions we will cover in this section. It will serve as a yardstick to judge how well your use of an LMS will meet your most pressing training needs.

Question One: Will Your LMS Provider Deliver the Support You Need?

A good LMS delivers remarkable benefits. It will track your courses, monitor who is taking and completing them, serve as a communications hub between your company and your learners, and do much more.

But an LMS is more than an app or software that you install and then walk away from. If you don't have an experienced learning management systems provider who can set up and fine-tune your LMS to meet your needs, you will never enjoy all the benefits of using it. So be sure to engage with a training company, like Tortal Training, that has the experience and staff to be with you every step of the way.

Question Two: How Will You Determine What You Need Your LMS to Do for You?

As we discussed earlier in this section, there was a reason that motivated you to make the decision to start using an LMS for monitoring and maximizing your training. And as we suggested, it is critically important to keep that reason in mind.

But there is something else to consider . . .

You might not know everything that an LMS can do for you

Yes, you know that you need one. But chances are you will only come to understand everything an LMS can do for you after you have worked with a training expert to design and shape the LMS you will use. Did you know, for example, that an LMS can monitor the training that your employees are taking on their mobile phones? Or that after training is over, it can deliver reminders and new training concepts by sending text messages? Or that at least one LMS (the one developed by Tortal Training) allows you to update and adapt older training materials yourself?

That is one reason to work with an experienced LMS development company. If you don't, you will probably be missing some key benefits that you didn't know existed.

Question Three: How Much Control Does Your New LMS Allow You Over Content?

You might think that an LMS serves as little more than a front page that your employees can visit when they want to pick a training course and sign up for it.

In reality, an LMS is much more powerful than that. It allows your company to decide who can enroll in which courses (perhaps your salespeople will only be allowed to take your most advanced selling course after they have completed earlier courses), who has permission to modify and write course content, and even who has permission to simply *view* your course content.

Because your LMS is much more than a shopping list of courses, be sure to ask your LMS provider about how you can monitor permissions.

Question Four: Who Is Going to Know How to Use Your LMS?

Your LMS should be supported by administrators who have been trained to support both your LMS and the employees who use it. So . . . who will those administrators be? You might say, "Somebody in HR." But stop and think, are there people in your HR department who have the time and bandwidth to answer questions like these on a daily basis?

- "I was taking my course yesterday and got up to Unit Six, but now I can't find the course and start again from there."
- "I am trying to enroll in Inventory Management Training, but the LMS seems to have no record of me as a user."
- "No one here in our training center in Cleveland can log in today . . . why?"

Once your LMS is up and running, chances are it will be running smoothly and relatively trouble-free. But issues do come up and unless you have administrators who can step in, you could end up with trainees who are under-supported . . . and frustrated and locked out.

Question Five: How Powerful Are the Reporting Features of Your LMS?

You need it to provide instant data on how many people are enrolled in each of your training courses, how far along they are with their training courses, how they have done on tests and quizzes, and more. An LMS that makes it difficult to access reports, or that doesn't provide up-to-date information in the format you need, will not be doing the job for you.

Question Six: How Will Your LMS Grow?

You might decide that you will set up your LMS to monitor and manage participation in five different training courses. Those are your plans for the moment but stop and think. If you decide to add five more courses over the next year, what should you do today to be sure that your LMS will be able to expand in the months and years ahead to meet your future needs? And to meet them smoothly, and without costing a lot in future fees?

If you build and set up your LMS in the right way today, growing it in the future will be both easier and less expensive. That means working with a highly experienced LMS company like Tortal Training.

Have More Questions? Contact a Tortal Learning Developer Today

Tortal is a leading LMS developer and enabler for a very simple reason . . .

LMS development and implementation is central to what we do . . . it is part of our training DNA!

When the time is right for you to start enjoying the benefits of using an LMS, Tortal is the right training development company to call.

Eight Critical Questions to Ask when Selecting an LMS

You visit the website of a company that offers a Learning Management System and it looks terrific. There are screenshots of menus and reports, images of people who are happily learning, and quotes from delighted users. It looks good.

But should that level of information convince you that you have found the LMS that meets your needs? Not really. And if you start using that LMS and it doesn't work for you, how much time and money will you lose?

You can prevent mistakes by applying a process of due diligence when you select an LMS. Here are eight critical questions to ask.

1) Does the LMS support the training you currently offer . . . and that you will offer in the future?

If you are currently providing just one training program for 15 call-center employees and only need to track enrollments and course completions, that is one thing. If you offer six courses to 100 product installers and you want to know how well they scored on embedded quizzes and monitor other data, that is another.

So in addition to reviewing the LMS as it is described online, speak with a representative of the company that offers the LMS to be sure you are buying one with features that can expand to meet your needs.

2) Does the LMS pass a road test?

Test the fundamental functions you will use. Try to enroll some employees – how easy is that to do? Try to upload and organize your course content – again, how easy is that to do? Try to generate the reports you will need after you are using the LMS – again, is it easy to do that? If an LMS is difficult to use, the time to learn that is before you sign up and start paying for it.

3) Do your people like it?

Be sure to get evaluation and feedback from the people who will actually use the LMS. Does it meet their needs? Those people should include the members of your training team, managers who supervise the employees who will be trained, and a cross-section of people who will take the training.

4) How easy is it to find answers and get help if problems arise?

Are there FAQs and information resources that users can access on their own? If a user needs help with a problem, how quickly can they get support? Because your training operation can stop while you wait for a service ticket to be handled, test drive support by posting a question, or call the service number, and see what happens. If you can't get immediate or prompt help, it's best to move on and consider other LMS systems.

5) Can the LMS grow with your future training needs?

The system that is right for you today might not be right tomorrow. So in addition to speaking with someone from the LMS provider about your current courses, be sure to discuss new courses you will offer in the future and other possible changes in your training. If you plan to double the number of your training programs or the size of your workforce, will the LMS accommodate those changes?

6) Can you see a live, complete demonstration of product features?

It is tempting to pick an LMS quickly, by watching three-minute videos that are on the LMS provider's website. But because you are investing in a product that you will be using for years, you are entitled to experience a personalized product demonstration, either face-to-face with a company representative or in a video meeting. If a company is unwilling to spend that time with you, how willing will it be to provide support when you need it later on? Not very.

7) Can you talk with no fewer than three current users?

They can provide you with a greater depth of information than the "we love it!" quotes that the LMS provider puts on its website. So be sure to speak with no fewer than three current users and ask them:

- Why did you choose this LMS?
- How many steps were required to set up your training before you could fully use it?

- Did the LMS meet all your needs? If not, what was missing?
- When you have a problem or a question, how do you request help, and how long does it typically take before your issue is resolved?
- Do you expect to keep using this LMS in the future?

8) How experienced is the provider?

You don't want to be only the second or third client who has used the company's LMS product. You want a training development company that has extensive experience setting up and supporting its LMS product. Here are some questions to ask:

- How many companies are currently using your LMS?
- Do you have clients who have set up training that is similar to ours?
- Based on your experience, what do you think the steps will be to get us up and running?
- Do you foresee any obstacles or special challenges in getting us up and running, and how do you think you can overcome them?

And be sure to check out the company's reviews online!

How to Get the Most from a Mobile Learning Management System

If you are already using a Learning Management System – and you should be – you are already enjoying a number of benefits. You know how many of your employees are enrolled in each of your training courses at any time. You know who has completed those courses, and how well they have done on embedded quizzes. And when courses are done, you can easily follow up with your trainees by emailing them additional course units, reminders to use what they learned in training, and lots of encouragement.

But have you taken the way you use your LMS to a higher level, by. . .

Using your LMS to monitor and manage training that you deliver to your employees on their mobile devices?

The Many Benefits of Training on Mobile Devices

Before we explore the pluses of using an LMS to monitor your mobile training, let's ask two basic questions. *First*, are you training your employees on mobile devices? And *second*, could offering mobile training solve any of the bottlenecks you are currently facing in your training?

Mobile training can be just the solution you are looking for if you are facing challenges like these . . .

- **Your employees work in multiple locations** and it is impractical to have them all travel to a central training center.

- **You are about to introduce a new product or service and** need to train a large number of employees about it quickly.

- **You are opening a number of new businesses** – you're expanding! – and need to train lots of employees quickly.

- **You hire a number of employees** for short periods of time to fill specific staffing needs. *Example:* You need to staff a number of gardening supply stores for the summer months only, and usually hire students who you need to train quickly.

- **You have older training materials –** maybe printed booklets or tests – and need an effective way to update and disseminate them quickly to a large number of workers.

- **You need to update your training materials often.** Mobile training programs can be updated quickly by your training team, which can also produce multiple versions of the same training materials for use in different regions, or even in different languages.

- **You can foresee that mobile training will deliver more training at a lower cost.** Not many people realize that mobile training can deliver cost savings. When you already have a training program in your system, rolling it out to new employees will cost very little money. And if you need to update a mobile training course, you and your training designers can typically get the job done quickly, at less cost than creating a new course "from the ground up." So remember that mobile training can save you a lot of money in design costs.

- **You can offer instant, pinpointed training when you need it.** If one of your company locations is hiring, new employees can be trained immediately – just hand them a tablet or let them log on using their phones. There is no longer a need to schedule a day of training in your company learning center.

But Can You Make Mobile Training Work? Five Issues to Think About

Mobile training is just the solution to challenges like those. But despite the fact that mobile training can solve those problems remember that it is not a "magic bullet." You cannot just create courses for delivery on mobile devices and sit back and wait for great training to happen.

To make mobile training work, you have to solve some practical problems like these . . .

1. **How many of the employees you will train already have mobile devices?** And if they do, can you require them to use their own devices to complete their training? In many

cases, you can. But if your labor pool is made up of individuals who do not own smartphones, or whose data plans will not provide the extra bandwidth they need to take your training, you will have to find another way. One is to equip your additional locations with tablets that employees can use to take your courses. *Tip:* Remember to structure your courses so your employees will need to log on with their own credentials; if you don't, you will have no way to track the training they have taken or use your LMS to monitor their progress.

2. **Do you have good Wi-Fi in the locations where your employees will train?** Chances are you do, but be sure to find out before you take your mobile training live.

3. **Will you expect your employees to take their training at home or in other non-work locations?** If you will, how will that requirement be affected by considerations #1 and #2, described just above?

4. **Can the kind of training you need be deliverable on mobile devices?** Yes, mobile devices are pretty powerful. But let's face the fact that they are little and that if your training is highly interactive (requiring trainees to respond to questions via a touch interface), delivery to smartphones might not offer the right kind of training experience. Tablets might work better. Again, you should consider this issue before

deciding that mobile training is the best option for your training needs.

5. **Have you thought about security issues?** Be sure to speak with an experienced training development company about this issue. Do you really want your employees to be sitting in Starbucks locations while they take your training on their phones, for example? If an employee loses his or her phone and someone else picks it up, what risks will that present to your company? There are steps you can take, like requiring employees to log in before starting to train and having training sessions time out after a few minutes if the user has been idle. But be sure to consider cybersecurity as you plan your mobile training.

The Benefits of Using an LMS to Manage Mobile Training

After you have addressed those caveats and considerations, you can focus on creating strong mobile training programs and using your LMS to track their use. If you are not sure how that might work, why not speak with a Tortal Training Expert today, and learn more about Tortal's LMS? Call (704) 323-8953.

How will you benefit from integrating your mobile training with your LMS? Here are some advantages to consider . . .

- **You will be able to know who is taking your mobile training,** how much of it they have completed, how they have performed on embedded quizzes, and more.

- **Your employees will be more engaged** and will learn more. A mobile LMS allows you to communicate directly with trainees to deliver messages like, "You just completed Unit 3. You are a star!" and, "If you start Unit 4 today, we have a complimentary Starbucks card for you!"

- **More of your employees** will complete their training. Why? Because if one worker pauses for a day after completing one unit, your LMS will alert you and send an automated email to that worker to say, "Don't forget to jump back on and complete Unit 4!"

- **You can automate the delivery** of additional training units. Every two weeks, your employees can receive a new training unit on their phones, or at any interval you decide.

- **You can onboard new employees** more easily, thanks to mobile training. And thanks to your LMS, that process can be recorded immediately in new employees' HR files.

- **Your advanced training** will attract better employees to your company. When you can tell prospective employees that you offer advanced, mobile-delivered training, they become more motivated to work for you.

Why? Because when applicants hear that your company is offering training that will help them learn and succeed, they become more likely to see your company as an employer of choice. And they will tell other people, and word will get around that you are a forward-thinking company that trains its employees.

- **And you may be able to monitor what is happening** . . . using your own mobile device. It's another benefit of using your LMS. Be sure to talk about that when you speak with a Tortal Training advisor about how your mobile training can work with your LMS to deliver better training.

Integrate Your Mobile Training with Your LMS . . . and Succeed!

Thanks to your LMS and mobile training, you can become a company that trains consistently, immediately and regularly. The result? You build a more skilled, more agile workforce that helps you build your competitiveness.

Part Nine: Secret Sauce Strategies from Our Top Training Designers

Here's a powerful strategy you can start using today.

How are training and coaching different?

- **Training** is all about teaching needed skills, knowledge and attitudes to groups of people.
- **Coaching** is delivered by one coach or mentor to one employee at a time. Its goal is to help individual employees grow, perform better, and succeed.

When used alongside training, coaching can develop top performers who can lead your organization to new levels of success.

Motivational Questions that Coaching Can Answer

Effective coaches help employees discover answers to questions like these:

- "What should my very next position be in this company, and what can I do now to prepare for it?"
- "What career paths would be good for me to consider and pursue in this company?"
- "What specific skills and traits do I need to do my job better and move up in the organization?"
- "How can I manage my time better, get more done, and focus on more important activities?"
- "Are there specific communication skills, like better listening, that I need to develop?"
- "Should I go back to school to add certain skills or credentials?"

Setting Up an Effective Coaching Program

Here are some steps that can help your coaching program succeed:

- **In general, coaches should hold higher management positions than the people they are coaching.** This incentivizes employees to participate fully, because they sense they are getting advice from people who understand what it takes to assume high-level roles in your company.
- **Don't have employees coached by their immediate supervisors.** There are many reasons. One is that you want employees to feel free to explore areas where they need to improve, and those conversations are more likely to take place when the coach is someone from another department, division, or even a company office that is located in a different part of the country.
- **Set out specific expectations for what you would like coaching to accomplish.** Tell employees in writing what's in it for them. They can learn better time-management skills, for example, identify paths to advancement in your company or enjoy other specific benefits.
- **Coach your coaches.** Instead of assuming that they have what it takes to be good coaches, train them to handle the role effectively. A training development company like Tortal Training can be your best partner in that process. We also recommend books like *Mentoring 101* by the leadership expert John Maxwell and *The Mentor's Guide* by Lois J. Zachary.

- **Keep HR and coaching separate.** To encourage learners to openly explore areas where they need development, make it clear that reports on coaching progress will not be filed in their personnel folders in HR or explored in depth during performance reviews. Your coaching program should be something different that stands apart.
- **Offer coaching to as many employees as you can.** You don't want certain employees to feel discouraged because they have not been selected for coaching, while their peers have. Another benefit of coaching large groups of employees is that you can unexpectedly discover and develop new stars. If you didn't coach them, you might never recognize their abilities.

Why Training + Coaching = Great Employee Development

When employees are *trained* to do their jobs well and also *coached* to be the best they can be, you'll be on your way to creating tomorrow's stars in your organization.

Use the ADDIE Framework to Design Better Training

Since the ADDIE training model was developed at Florida State University in 1975, training designers have added their own tweaks and improvements to the way it works.

But despite all the refinements over the years, ADDIE is still worth knowing about. It provides a useful structure for planning, revising and implementing your training. Let's review the steps today and see what we can learn.

Meet ADDIE

ADDIE is an acronym that divides the process of training into the following steps:

- **Step One: Analyze** your business needs and consider what kind of training will support them. Weigh who your learners are, pinpoint the behaviors you want your training to change, develop metrics to measure, and plan an overall timeline for training.
- **Step Two: Design** a master plan. In this step, you decide how your trainees prefer to learn, where and how your training will be delivered (in classrooms, computerized learning centers, on mobile devices or tablets) and what kind of training materials will work best (videos, training manuals, interactive quizzes, etc.).
- **Step Three: Develop** your training materials. In this phase, your instructional designers create the lesson plan and materials you will use.

- **Step Four: Implement** your plan in the strongest way you can. This usually takes place in two steps. First, you train your trainers to use the materials you have developed in the preceding phases. Second, you launch your program.
- **Step Five: Evaluate** the success of your training, in several ways. One goal is to loop back to Step One (Analyze) to see whether your training has gotten you closer to meeting your business objectives. A second step is to measure and monitor your metrics to see whether your program has changed behaviors and achieved its goals. The third step is to evaluate your training plan, materials and trainers to find ways to improve your overall training initiative.

Think of ADDIE as a Way to Plan and Evaluate Results

While not set in stone, the ADDIE framework offers a good checklist for training. As we noted at the start of today's post, it has been refined over the years. If you're planning new training that achieves results, we invite you to speak with a Tortal Training consultant today.

Supercharge Your Training by Asking for Feedback from Trainees

It's standard practice to hand out survey forms when a day of training is done, or to email feedback forms to trainees the next day. But is that enough?

Probably not. Because getting the right feedback in the right ways can lead to continuous improvement in all your training efforts, let's take a closer look at how to add value to the feedback process.

Collect *Operational Feedback* as Soon as Sessions End

It is too early to collect data on the long-term effects that your training could produce. But it is a great time to ask trainees to comment on the quality of the program, by asking questions like these:

- Did you learn what you expected to in the training sessions?
- Was the trainer knowledgeable, prepared, and able to answer questions and resolve any problems?
- Did the training keep you interested and engaged?
- Which concepts do you think will be the most helpful and productive?
- How soon will you start to apply the ideas that you took away?
- Was there a good mixture of presentations, breakout sessions and other forms of learning?

- Did any problems occur during the session? If so, how were they resolved?
- What was the best part of the program?
- What part of the program needed the most improvement?
- What suggestions would you like to make about future training?

Ask about *Results* at Regular Intervals after Training

Collect a different kind of feedback in the weeks and months after training is done – feedback that lets trainees tell you about results. Here are some questions to ask:

- Have you been able to apply what you learned?
- Specifically, which ideas have you put into practice?
- Have you been unable to apply some of the ideas you learned? If so, what were they, and why?
- Can you provide any specific feedback on how your activities have changed since training? Have you closed more sales or accomplished other measurable results?
- In light of what you now know, what changes would you recommend in future training programs?

Compare Feedback against *Measurable Metrics*

Compare the feedback to the metrics that you developed before training began. Remember that feedback from trainees generally yields "soft" data; they think they have applied certain concepts or that they are being more productive. But it is not enough to have people feel better, you need to quantify training results against hard data like increased sales, higher levels of customer satisfaction and cost savings.

Build Feedback into Training and Boost Your ROI

If you would like to know more about using feedback to augment the effectiveness of your training, give Tortal Training a call today at 704-323-8953.

Should you offer incentives to the employees who are taking part in your training, or who complete it successfully?

"What a great idea," one trainer tells us. "Some organizations forget to incentivize people for using what they learn in training programs, but it can be a very effective way to reinforce learning."

Yet we've heard some dissenting opinions too. "I think it's redundant," a sales trainer says. "When people start applying what they learned, the benefits should be self-rewarding in terms of closing more sales, earning bigger commissions and helping the company succeed."

Who Is Right?

While there is a kernel of truth in what the "redundant" trainer is saying, we know the "great idea" commentator is right. "Mr. Redundant," we think, is misunderstanding what incentives can be and how they can augment training.

Here are some ways to create and use incentives to increase your training results and ROI:

- **Make incentives ongoing and meaningful.** We have seen trainers hand out key chains and t-shirts at the close of training sessions. There's nothing wrong with that – it's a nice and motivational thing to do – but it only produces lasting effects if more incentives are delivered strategically over time. For example, you can

205

reward employees every time they complete future training lessons, modules and courses.

- **Use technology to deliver rewards.** If your employees are doing their training on mobile phones, you can deliver a prepaid restaurant or store coupon to them after they complete each unit. Delivery can be automated, built right into your training program.
- **Don't shy away from big rewards and prizes.** Family vacation packages for employees can work well to motivate them to sell the most of a new product in a specific period of time after they have been trained to sell it, for example. (Just be sure to clearly explain the rules: exactly how much they need to sell, the precise closing date and time when the competition ends, how many of the incentives will be offered, etc. Spelling out the specifics prevents later misunderstandings or hurt feelings.)
- **Remember that simple encouragement can be a great incentive too.** A personalized note or email of encouragement or thanks from a company leader can be a great motivator – and it doesn't cost a penny. Remember, however, that effective motivational communications are specific, not general. *Example:* An email that says, "Congratulations Bob on bringing in 25 new clients by using our new marketing platform" is more powerful that a generic message that only says, "Thank you for trying our new marketing platform."
- **Honors and recognition are effective incentives too.** If certain employees achieve excellent results by using your training, you can invite them to join a new Training Advisory

Panel, an Honors Circle or other committee that you have created.

- **Use incentives to encourage feedback in the months after training is completed.** Employees might (or might not) respond to an email that says, "Please let us know how you are using what you learned in our training program last month." But chances are good that they will respond if you offer even a small incentive. Prepaid restaurant and store coupons are good choices here too.
- **Offer incentives for suggestions.** They are an effective way to solicit feedback for improving future training. The result can be continuous improvement that leads to better and better training results and ROI.

Our CEO Evan Hackel believes that one key to building retention, performance and satisfaction is to tell job applicants what will be expected of them if they come on board – and even to tell them during interviews. "Why wait until the first job review and then tell employees what they haven't done right?" Evan wrote in a recent article. And we couldn't agree more.

It makes sense to utilize the earliest opportunities to explain the behaviors, attitudes and accomplishments that your organization values. For example, you can tell job applicants, "We value and reward people who can quickly apply creative solutions to customer issues, who are eager to contribute new ideas and solutions and above all, who demonstrate a strongly positive attitude toward each other and our clients."

Training Offers an Opportunity to Set Motivational Expectations

The training you deliver to new employees offers an opportunity to teach not only skills, but what is valued in your organization. Here are some opportunities . . .

- **Talk about the values and behaviors** that bring success in your company.
- **Discuss your company's vision,** mission and values. As an exercise, have each employee explain, in his or her own words, just what the company vision is.

- **Use videos and other engaging content** that teach compelling lessons about your company's values. You can tell the company story and profile top executives, customers and employees who are really getting the job done.
- **Explain advancement opportunities** and career paths within your organization. Spelling out this information motivates employees much more effectively than letting them discover "the ropes" after they come on board.
- **Use games, exercises,** and break-out activities that encourage trainees to think about *why* they are performing activities, not simply trying to learn the steps you expect them to take.

Get More from Training by Teaching Industry-Specific Terms and Acronyms

If you take a moment to think back on the last few meetings you've attended, you will remember all the industry-specific terms, abbreviations and acronyms that were flying around the room. Now try to imagine how much you would have understood or contributed if you had no idea what all that "lingo" meant. And imagine what could happen if your employees finished your training programs without learning what those terms mean. Would your salespeople be able to discuss customer needs effectively and close sales? Would new managers be able to communicate effectively with vendors, company outsiders – or even the people they supervise?

There are other benefits to including current terms in your training too. While you are planning your training programs, it pays you to ask, "What are the latest terms we need to talk about?" That question can help you quickly uncover any "thin" training areas that you might have been overlooking, such as new technologies and trends.

Use Professional Journals and Organizations to Identify the Terms You Need to Teach

Of course you know most of the new terms and acronyms that other professionals are currently using in your industry. But to be sure you are not overlooking any new jargon, review these sources too:

- **Industry-specific journals** that are widely read in your field.
- **Programs for conferences and trade shows,** where keynoters and other presenters are discussing the latest need-to-know trends and terms.

Build Critical Terms into Your Training

If you are looking for a training development company, be sure to ask whether their training materials and course content can be customized to include the latest industry information and terminology. Remember that even off-the-shelf training products should be customizable to meet your needs.

Part Ten: The Critical Link Between Training and Your Brand

Have you ever had an experience like one of these?

- **You were impressed by the service-oriented salespeople** at the appliance store where you bought your new stove. But the people who came to deliver and install it were hurried and couldn't answer your questions. Plus, they tracked dirt into your house.
- **You visited a fast food restaurant** and tried to order a special sandwich that you saw advertised on television the night before. But when you walked up to the counter to order it, the server didn't know what it was and had to ask the manager if it was available.
- **You got an email flyer from a tire store** that showed a young technician in a spotless uniform who was ready to check your tires and rotate them for free. But when you visited a local branch of the store, a grumpy guy behind the counter seemed to be too busy to talk to you.

If you've had that kind of experience, you've dealt with a company that has failed to understand that every person in an organization – from the CEO to the front line employee – has a role to play in making good on the brand promise and delivering the brand experience.

Training Is the Solution

The most effective way to inspire a brand commitment to excellence is to ensure that every employee in your organization understands his or her unique function in communicating and supporting your brand, and why it's important. The right kind of training processes can create a company full of "brand stewards" who take your vision as seriously as you do.

When employees understand the "why" behind what they're asked to do, they are empowered to take ownership. Their willing cooperation frees up their creative energy so they can apply it to making your brand stronger. For instance, it was a McDonald's employee who came up with the idea to start serving breakfast. It was a Subway employee's idea to bake fresh bread onsite. Both those activities are now iconic parts of each brand experience – and they came from employees in the ranks.

In both cases, the employees understood the brand goals and used their creativity to help further the cause. If you want to create an environment where people not only buy in and do the right things, but actually add to the collective vision of what your brand can be, it's vital that you have the right kind of brand training in place.

Tell Your Company Story to Add Depth to Your Training

If you were creating a training program for Apple, would you fail to mention Steve Jobs? If you were designing training for Walmart sales associates, would you forget to mention Sam Walton – the visionary company founder who reinvented customer service? And if you were training personnel to work at Disney theme parks, would you leave out Mickey Mouse, Minnie Mouse . . . or Walt himself?

Of course not. Their stories are part of the DNA that lives on in the companies they founded. And what about your company's DNA? Who was your founder, for example, and what prompted him or her to start the firm? Every company, including yours, has a story. It was started with a purpose, it has a reason for being and it has a story that should be told.

If you take even a little time to talk about your founders and your history – especially when training new employees – your training immediately improves, for some very practical reasons.

- **Employees immediately become a team.** They're no longer people who just show up and start working. They understand that they are part of something that is bigger, and that adds conviction to what they do.

- **They immediately learn important lessons about company values and priorities.** Maybe you work for a bank that was founded after World War II to help returning soldiers buy their first homes or open new businesses. Or perhaps 150 years ago your founder invented a piece of equipment that turned your region into a center of agriculture. Or your founder is a social activist who launched your company with a big idea to help the world. Those are important stories. Whatever yours is, why not take a little time to tell it in your training? The lessons people learn are more than nice to know – they train employees how to make practical decisions that are in line with company values and ethics.
- **They gain a repertoire of stories to take out with them into the world.** Salespeople gain the ability to talk about your company, its founders, and what you stand for. Executives can talk about your company with pride when they interact with leaders of other companies. Even customer service representatives and other front-line personnel can project deeply held company values and attitudes.

And here's another training tip . . .

Why tell your company story with words alone, when historical photos of your founder or early company facilities can give trainees a compelling sense of how your firm got started? Images offer a powerful way to turn "dry history" into more powerful training.

Why You Should Talk about Your Brand During Training

Employee training, and onboarding training especially, can do more than teach your workers the skills they need to do their jobs. Training can also teach your team about your brand. In fact, if you train new employees without explaining what your brand is or why your company is exceptional, you are missing an opportunity to not only train your workers, but to energize them.

How should you talk about your brand? Here are some topics to consider weaving into your training.

- **Advancement** – Do you offer good employees the opportunity to stay with you for the long term, take on new responsibilities, and succeed?
- **Attitude** – Are you a company that values energy, positivity, optimism, and cooperation?
- **Benefits** – What extras do you offer that make your company an exceptional place to work, like a good health care plan, flextime, exercise facilities, on-site childcare, and other benefits that are part of your value system?
- **Case studies** – What stories can you tell about past successes that have been important markers on your road to success?
- **Communications** – Is your company a place where employees' ideas are welcomed, utilized and rewarded?

- **Customers –** Who do you serve, and what do you give them that serves their needs?
- **Differentiators –** What makes your company different, and better, from your competitors?
- **Employees –** Do you have employees who can tell motivational stories about why they love to work for you?
- **Facilities and resources –** What is special and unique about your headquarters and other locations?
- **Family –** How does your company work hard to create a healthy work/life balance for all your employees?
- **Future plans –** Where are you planning to go in the future as a company, and how are you planning to get there?
- **History –** What is unique about your company's past that makes it exceptional?
- **Inclusiveness –** Are you a company that welcomes and makes a home for people from all backgrounds?
- **Leaders –** Who founded your company, who leads it now? Have certain current or past employees become champions of what you do and how you do it?
- **Logos, colors, and visual elements –** Can you showcase them in a motivational way during your training?
- **Products and services –** What products have become the foundation of your success? What is unique and different about them?

- **Regional values** – Is your company a leading citizen of your community, state, or region . . . and how do you serve in exceptional ways?
- **Safety** – Is your company an especially safe and secure place for people to work?
- **Technology** – Do you offer the latest and best technology for your employees to learn and use, and how do both your employees and your customers benefit?
- **Training** – Do you invest in exceptional training that helps employees do their jobs exceptionally well and succeed?
- **Value as an employer** – How and why is your company an exceptionally good place to work?

Remember, Branding Is More than a Marketing Tool

It would not be an exaggeration to say that your brand is your heartbeat, your soul, your unique value . . . and more. Be sure to make it an important component of your training.

Train Your People to Tell the World about Your Brand

A consistent brand identity is the glue that connects every piece of your customer's experience. From initial contact, to point of sale, to ongoing engagement, every touchpoint is a chance to fulfill your brand's unique promise. Without that kind of consistency, your customers can feel disconnected from your brand, and ultimately, hesitate to buy or become repeat customers. And training is the best place to get your people on board with your brand.

Let's Look at Some Great Brands

Let's stop to consider companies that have used powerful branding to build their success:

- **Meineke® uses the brand message "Taking Care of Your Car Shouldn't Take Over Your Life®"** to let customers know that the company saves time, relieves worry, and makes life simpler.
- **L. Bean's famous "Guaranteed to Last®" brand promise** is communicated on the company website, in product packaging and shipping documents, in company stores, in calling centers, and in every other interaction with customers. Customers know that if an L.L. Bean product ever fails, they can return it, no questions asked.
- **BMW has long promised to build "The Ultimate Driving Machine®,"** and uses that brand message consistently in advertising, social media and other contact points.

- **The Walt Disney Company's promise of "Timeless Family Entertainment"** is communicated by company employees at theme parks, retail outlets and all other customer contact points.

How do you train your employees to support, communicate and strengthen your brand in every customer interaction?

Make a Commitment to Train Your Employees to Become "Brand Stewards"

When designing training, most companies tend to jump immediately to identifying processes to be improved. Many miss the opportunity to train their people – beginning when they are new hires – to act as great stewards of their brands.

The message? Whether you are developing training in-house or working with a training development company, look for opportunities to engage people with your brand. Remember that videos that tell your company's values and mission can be a great and time-efficient way of letting trainees know who you are and what your stand for.

Put a New Company-Wide Emphasis on Branding

A strong and compelling brand promise should be consistently lived and communicated in every corner of your organization, not only taught to trainees. To make your brand promise genuine and compelling:

- **Work with your marketing and advertising managers** to move your brand messaging front and center.
- **Encourage your company** leaders to talk about what your brand is and what it stands for.
- **Communicate your brand promise** in your website content, social media channels, printed company materials – and everywhere else. Use company videos, customer testimonials and other media effectively.
- **Develop company mission statements** and vision statements that clearly express your brand values.
- **Encapsulate your brand promise** into clear and simple words that your employees can use when interacting with customers and stakeholders. Think of these words as "elevator speeches" that all your staffers can use to trumpet your unique brand promise to the world.

Part Eleven: Training for Franchise Success

Why You Should Provide Great Training at Your
Franchise Convention

Your convention is a great place to train current
franchisees and onboard new ones too.

Everyone in your organization – or most of them –
are in one place at one time, which offers you a
significant opportunity to educate them effectively,
consistently, and compellingly. Yet what kind of
training should you provide? And how should you
deliver it?

Those are critical questions. Let's take a closer
look.

Motivate Your Owners and Fire Them Up to Succeed

You have concrete skills that you would like to
teach everyone, of course. And it is important to
cover them at your franchise conference. At the
same time, it would be a mistake to cover only
"hard skills" and tasks, while ignoring entirely the
opportunity to get your franchisees excited and
motivated to succeed.

Many training opportunities offer a chance to
motivate and inspire your franchise owners, at
your annual franchise conference, including:

**Inspiring keynotes and speeches given by exciting
motivational speakers.** The right keynote from the
right speaker can energize your attendees right at
the start of your convention. The result can be that

they will be more motivated to learn what you want them to . . . and more likely to apply what they learned after your convention is over. When selecting a keynoter, keep these considerations in mind:

- **The keynote speaker should have a message and a personality that "fit" in your industry and resonate with your owners.** You should stop and think carefully as you consider which speakers to use. Even some good-looking, experienced speaker might not be right for all your franchisees. At one franchise conference a few years ago, for example, the keynoter was a well-known football coach whose energetic talk fell short with the 50% of the franchisees who were not sports fans. So as you watch videos of speakers you are considering, keep asking, "Is this right for our audience?" Another approach is to send your franchisees links to videos from the speakers you are considering, and to invite them to vote on whom they will hear.
- **Consider having your founder, CEO or another one of your top executives offer the keynote or lead key sessions.** Do this only if he or she is a strong speaker who is able to make a compelling presentation. But if one member of your top team fills the bill regarding those skills, he or she could be a great choice to fire up your people and get them motivated.
- **Have your most enthusiastic and successful franchise owners give a panel presentation and tell their success stories.** If they are

fired up about being part of your family, they will inspire your other franchisees too.

Teach Current and New Owners about Your Brand

In training sessions, let people know who your company is and how you go about doing business. In other words, train them to understand that they are part of an important brand that lends value to their businesses. Some ways to present your brand include:

- **Show videos about your company that tell your story.** These videos could tell the story of the individual who founded your company, the history of the product or service that built your success, which profile your owners, employees and most important customers.
- **Have interactive training sessions where your franchisees discuss what your brand is, and what it means to your customers.** Your convention is a place where teams are born – teams that are made up of strong brand champions and ambassadors. Be sure to take advantage of this valuable, once-a-year opportunity.

Train Your People on Your Franchise Manual and System

Ample research has shown that when the majority of franchisees adhere closely to the instructions and systems that are laid out in their franchise's operations manual, that franchise becomes impressively more successful and profitable. When individual franchisees go their own way, the integrity of the brand suffers, for reasons like these:

- **Customers** don't know exactly what they can expect when they visit different locations.
- **Individual franchisees** use different vendors and even sell different products, which creates a situation that is difficult for the parent franchisor to control.
- **Signage and displays** are not used uniformly throughout the company, which can affect sales and the core business proposition.

Your convention offers an opportunity to prevent issues like those. In presentations, be sure to explain not only what rules franchisees are expected to follow, but why. When they come to view your manual and required activities as opportunities to sell more and increase profits, your entire franchise will benefit and become more profitable.

Train Your Franchisees on Key Functions

If you are currently using unified Point of Sale (POS) systems, for example, your convention offers an ideal setting to train people how to use them. The same is true if you want all your franchisees to use company displays and signage properly.

And then there are other key functions you should provide training for, depending on what services or products your franchise provides:

- **If you sell food or beverages,** you can train your franchisees to observe proper protocols for food preparation, storage, and maintenance of food preparation areas.
- **If you provide cleaning services or smoke remediation,** you can offer training on how business should be done.
- **If you are an automotive service franchise,** you can offer training on how to write service orders, how to upsell customers to higher-end tires and components, and more.
- **If you are a painting franchise,** you can offer training on how to prepare homes to be painted, how to remediate mold in interior areas, and other critical skills.

Remember that the vendors you use – the companies from which you buy the food you sell, the paint and cleaning products you use and other key supplies – are often able to provide presentations and training on how to use their products. And if you invite them to do so, the training they provide will be free.

Give Sales and Customer Service Training

No matter what business you are in, you are selling something, and you need to please customers.

Because these are two fertile areas for improvement in any franchise, consider offering focused training at your conference that can improve them.

Offer Onboarding Training

If you brought new franchisees into your franchise family in the last year, your annual conference is the ideal place to offer them special onboarding programs. You don't need to travel to visit them or have them visit your home office. Simply plan an afternoon of onboarding training on your key systems, bookkeeping protocols, HR basics and other fundamentals.

Introduce Distributed Training Programs at Your Conference

Do you offer training that your franchisees and their employees can take on their smartphones, tablets or other devices? If you do, how many of your people are using it? Your conference is a great setting to train everyone in your organization how to access and make the best use of the mobile training you offer.

Teach Your Franchisees to Use Your Learning Management System (LMS) If You Have One

Many companies today use sophisticated Learning Management Systems to track the training they provide. These systems allow companies to know how many employees have enrolled in training programs, how many have completed the programs they started, and more.

If you are currently using one of these programs, your annual conference offers the opportunity to train your owners how to use it. Just one training session can increase the number of locations that use your LMS.

Offer Informational Presentations on Real Estate and Insurance

These are core concerns for your franchisees! The good news is, real estate experts and insurance agents will often be willing to deliver talks at no charge for your franchise owners. Why? Because they might welcome business that your franchisees will bring to them.

Also Consider Giving Seminars on Accounting and Tax Law

If your franchise system uses a platform that tracks your franchisees' finances, you might not need to offer sessions on these topics. But if your franchisees are responsible for keeping their own books and preparing their own tax returns, informational sessions on these topics could be of great value to them.

In Summary:

If you want your annual conference to result in system-wide improvements that boost profits, result in happier franchisees, and more, the message is simple. Use your conference as a place to provide thoughtful and high-quality training experiences.

Use Training to Take Your Franchise from Good to Great

We have been in meetings where smart businesspeople plan how they will launch or expand their franchises.

A number of topics usually get discussed in those planning meetings. People ask, "Do we have a strong brand?" and "How is our signage?" and maybe even, "Do we have a good plan for recruiting new owners?" Yes, the questions go on and on. But many planners never get around to asking what the most critical question of all could be . . .

"Do we have phenomenal training in place to enable our expansion to succeed awesomely?"

You see, success of any franchise business depends on how well a company trains its new owners and further down the line, on how it trains employees who work at individual franchises. And that is true whether you are starting a new franchise company or growing one that already exists.

Your success depends on the training you provide, which means addressing these concerns as you plan your training.

Make Sure to Get Input from Everyone in Your Organization as You Plan Your Training

Everyone, including you, current franchise owners, and employees should help you define the specifics of what your training should cover. Even though you might be the owner or a highly ranked executive in the parent company, don't assume you know all the topics or skills your training should cover. You need to get input from everyone about what your training should be.

Create Role-Specific Training for the Jobs that Make Your Franchise Work

Many new or expanding franchise companies mistakenly believe that they only need to create training that tells new owners how to operate a franchise. They forget to identify other key jobs that make the business work, and they fail to create job-specific training for employees who fulfill other critical roles like selling on the retail floor or in the field, delivering and installing products, and more. So even though you might start by creating training for new franchise owners, go on to develop training for employees who perform all your most important functions.

Train New Owners How to Use Your Franchise System

There are many reasons why this is critically important. First and foremost, people buy franchises for the system! Also, you want owners to learn to benefit from the systems and support you have put in place for their benefit. On the subtler level, you want your franchise owners to tell prospective franchise owners that you provide industry-leading training and support that helped them succeed and become profitable from the day they opened their doors.

You also want franchises to grow because they have used the system, not because their owners used all kinds of tactics and strategies that they developed on their own; if a franchise grew because it adhered to the system and its rules, prospective buyers see that they can step in and start running their new businesses; all they have to do is stick with the system. Remember that buyers like the word, "Turnkey."

So when you train your system, you are building the value of your brand and your franchises, which makes your franchise company vastly more valuable in the marketplace.

Have Everyone in Your Organization Take and Fine-Tune the Training You Have Developed

How will they know what your training teaches unless they take it themselves? And how can they offer suggestions and revisions? If you have ever been in a situation where franchise owners "weigh in" and start to complain that training isn't teaching what it should, you know how important it is to get them to take the training and offer suggestions early on.

Let Prospective Franchise Owners Take the Training before They Buy

Training can be one of your most compelling tools for convincing new owners that your franchise is the one to buy, because you offer training that builds confidence, eliminates uncertainty, and minimizes the risk of failure. And after prospective buyers have taken your training, members of your sales team can call them to ask, "What did you think of our training . . . do you have any questions?" That's a natural and organic way to continue a conversation that helps prospective owners to make a buying decision.

Define Goals, Develop Metrics, Measure Results, and Keep Improving Your Training

How many of your new franchises are generating $1 million in sales during their first six months of operation? Is that figure ticking up or down, thanks to the training you offer? How many of your franchise owners purchase a second location in year two after they come on board? How many of them are using your marketing programs, and how - and how are those programs driving sales?

There are so many things to measure and, as the old saying goes, "How will you know what you are accomplishing if you never measure?" If you start your planning process by thinking not only about what you would like your training to accomplish, but how you will measure it, you will be taking a great first step toward creating training that moves the right needles and brings success to everyone in your franchise organization.

Want Stronger Franchise Development? Focus on an Amazing Franchise Operations and Training Program . . .

What do you see when you visit one of your franchise locations?

- *Do you see* a business where employees wear your uniform, where products are displayed using approved displays, and where you sense the power of your strong brand at work?
- *Or do you see* an operation where employees are wearing whatever they want, where many non-franchise-approved products and services are sold, where signage is not uniform, and where you get the feeling that you are visiting just any kind of company, not one that is part of your franchise family?

If you find yourself in that second kind of location, you are in a franchise where the owner has decided to ignore your systems and run the business as though it were his or her personal enterprise and not a franchise at all.

How serious a problem is that? It is a very serious problem indeed. Because when individual franchises are not run in compliance with your franchise's system and operations manual, your entire franchise becomes weaker, less profitable, and devalued in the marketplace. As a result, the growth of your franchise slows and stalls.

But when owners comply with your system, many good outcomes happen. Let's explore some of the reasons why.

When All Franchisees Use Your Systems . . .

- **Existing franchisees are great validators for your system,** because they can tell prospective owners, "This company has my back . . . it offers proven systems and training and a strong brand . . . it is a great franchise to own."
- **Existing franchisees are better able to expand in size and add new locations,** because they are utilizing proven tools that require less effort and investment on their part.
- **All your locations play a vital role** in supporting and building a unified and powerful brand.
- **Individual franchises become more profitable** by using the advertising and marketing programs that your parent company makes available to them.
- **Your franchisees are happier and make fewer costly mistakes** because they are using a proven system that has been tested.
- **Customers like to do business with you,** because they value working with a company that delivers a consistent and excellent customer experience.

How do you develop and deliver training that helps your current franchises grow and prosper, attracts new franchisees and supports system-wide development? Let's take a closer look.

Some Keys to a Training System that Supports Development and Growth

First, make sure training is part of your franchise culture . . .

That means writing it into the franchise's new mission and vision statements, talking about it at conferences and conventions, measuring who is taking the training, and comparing their performance to that of the people who are not. When training is part of the culture, franchisees understand that they are going to succeed as owners, even before they come on board.

Second, train from the business system . . .

A franchise organization is an operating system that contains information such as, "This is how we greet guests," "These are our values" and, "This is how we do things here." That system needs to be documented, typically in the form of an operations manual. But how do that system and those beliefs become alive? Through training. So when you are about to build training, look first to your system to determine what you are going to train on.

Third, don't try to teach everything immediately . . .

Many young franchise systems make this mistake. Their owners think, "We have great products, great marketing materials, great branding, a great system . . . and we are going to train everybody about every single piece of it all."

When franchises try to cram too much information into every learner's head, the result is like trying to get them to drink from a firehose. They cannot absorb everything, so they feel overwhelmed and actually learn less.

The solution is to think creatively and strategically about which things need to be trained, and when. What are the most important skills and knowledge to teach brand new owners? Which skills can be taught later, when owners have opened locations? Which concepts should be taught even later, when owners are staffing up, or getting involved in marketing and expanding?

Fourth, offer training in a blended fashion – in person and online . . .

Trainees absorb more information when you deliver it in several formats. You can, for example, use a professional speaker to motivate a class of new or current franchise owners, then provide instructor-led classroom training, and then continue to follow up with lessons your franchisees can take on tablet computers or smartphones.

A blended approach results in better learning and also allows you to deliver training effectively and economically to franchises in multiple locations.

Fifth, measure the results . . .

The only way to measure the results of your training is to identify metrics that you will measure before training starts, and after it is completed. What was the size of the average sale in your store before you provided sales training, for example, and how did that figure change after your sales training program? How many appliances were your installers able to install in a single day before they took your installation training, and how did that figure change in the weeks and months after training was over?

Measuring offers you the only way to understand the effectiveness of your training as well as the ROI you are getting from your training dollars.

Which Franchises Are the Most Likely to Thrive and Grow?

The most successful and durable franchises all share one trait. They have strong operational support and offer the best training.

Franchise Training . . . Why Franchisors Need to Provide Great training in their Systems

Franchise executives are among the smartest businesspeople anywhere. They need to master a range of disciplines that include entrepreneurship, branding, marketing, supply chain management, retail and POS technology, negotiating real estate deals, and many others.

But have you noticed that when it comes to training, even very capable franchise leaders sometimes seem to have blinders on? Some think of training as little more than an unavoidable cost of doing business. They want to provide just enough training to get their new franchise owners up to speed quickly, and not much more. And when it comes to helping their franchise owners train their employees, some don't want to become involved at all.

When you ask them about training, they are apt to make statements like these . . .

- "Our franchise owners have developed their own systems and solutions for doing business and don't want us to interfere."
- "Training is not worth spending a lot of money on   it's expensive and because staff turnover is high, you end up training people who leave."
- "We launched a new training program for our franchisees a few years ago, and only 10% of them signed up."
- "Training only pulls people away from their work, so profits fall."

When thinking like that sets in, negative things happen. Franchise leaders spend as little money as possible on training, nothing improves, and they seem to be happy with that. That is an immense mistake.

There is a better way. Let's look at some of the benefits that effective training can provide.

A Franchise that Has Well-Trained Owners and Employees Is Dramatically More Profitable

This is probably the most important, and most evident, benefit of offering good training to franchise owners and their employees. When they have the skills they need to operate a franchise's systems, there is less time lost, and profits rise. When they are trained to understand the products and services they offer, they sell more and provide a better level of customer service.

There are other benefits too. Better trained employees experience greater levels of job satisfaction, so they tend to stay with you longer. Through training, the entire enterprise operates more efficiently and generates greater profits.

Training Promotes Compliance

When individual franchise owners create their own systems for doing business, the entire franchise suffers. The brand becomes diluted and devalued. It also becomes more difficult for individual franchise owners to sell their locations to prospective owners, who are most likely to buy franchises that offer consistent and proven systems for doing business.

Training is the most effective way to assure compliance throughout a franchise. When a parent company provides excellent initial training and then follows up with additional training as needed, that company is taking a vital step toward assuring its own success.

Training Supports Expansion and Growth

If your franchise invests time and money to develop electronic training – including training that can be delivered on mobile devices and tablets - that training can be rolled out cost-effectively as a franchise expands to new locations.

The result? Your franchise can grow organically without having to develop new training courses and materials every time a growth phase occurs.

Training Encourages Owners to Operate their Franchises for Longer Periods of Time

When franchisees are trained to better execute your business plan, they sell more. That makes them happier, longer-lasting franchisees and helps to increase revenues.

Well-trained franchisees also enjoy greater operational efficiency, which further increases their profits. They become happier, sell more, and profit more. That is a win/win/win proposition for everyone.

Your Franchise Becomes More Attractive to New Owners

Prospective franchise owners are much more likely to buy franchises that offer them comprehensive training, for a very simple reason. They want to know that they will succeed as owners of a franchise because the franchise company "has their backs" and offers training to make sure they have the knowledge to succeed.

The best way to provide that level of confidence is to offer the kind of training that makes them say, "I can prosper in this franchise because it will train me to be successful. Plus, the risk of failure will be minimized."

It is an excellent idea to not only tell prospective buyers how good your training is, but to let them participate in your training programs while they are deciding whether or not to buy one of your franchises. When they experience how good your training is, they will be much more likely to buy.

Well-Trained Franchisees Become Better Validators

When a prospective franchise buyer calls one of your current franchise owners and asks, "Is this a good franchise to buy?" you want that owner to answer, "Yes! The franchisor provides great training and support." Remember that just one negative comment can prevent a prospective franchisee from buying - and you know the high cost of recruiting them and convincing them to buy. This is another payback that training offers you.

Training Prevents Franchises from Failing

Better profitability and training reduce the number of individual franchises that fail and close their doors. And when prospective buyers are looking at your franchise, they want to see that a very small number of locations have gone out of business. It's critical.

Who Needs Training?

Many franchise owners and top executives believe that training is something that should only be delivered to retail salespeople, product installers, call center representatives, service personnel, and other front-line employees who interact directly with customers.

While it is important to provide those front-line employees with training, a franchise can also benefit from training a wider range of personnel, who can include . . .

- **Individual franchise owners,** who are critically important professionals to train.
- **Executives and managers in franchise headquarters,** who can only benefit from improving their knowledge and skills in critical operational areas that are important throughout your franchise locations. One good approach is to have them take the same training that is being given to individual franchise owners and their

employees. In that way, personnel in headquarters stay acutely aware of what is really happening in every level of your enterprise.

- **Employees who work in individual franchises,** whose effectiveness has the biggest impact on the franchise's overall success.

How to Develop Cost-Effective Training for Your Franchise

Here are some steps to follow . . .

- **Identify jobs and positions** where improved performance promises to provide you with the greatest ROI on the investment you make in training. In a franchise system, for example, you might decide that your organization would profit most by investing in training for your salespeople, store supervisors, front-desk personnel, or product installers. Once you have identified these jobs, put them in priority order and then develop training for your top priorities first.
- **Carefully identify the specific tasks** that will bring about the greatest benefits in each job if you trained employees to perform them better. If you train your front-desk hotel staff to deliver better customer service, for example, how much benefit could you expect to receive? Or if you could train each of your retail salespeople to increase the size of each sale by 10%, how much impact will that have on your bottom

line? Remember to talk to the employees who are currently performing the functions where your training will focus. They are uniquely positioned to offer suggestions about which of their functions need improving and training.

- **Develop training that focuses on only** a select few of the skills that promise to deliver the most meaningful results if they were improved. Resist the temptation to try to develop a program that teaches dozens and dozens of concepts and skills. Experience shows that trainees retain and improve more if they are trained on only three or four main concepts in a training session. Remember, you can add more training modules later on.

- **Define metrics** for your training. Do you want your product installers to increase the quantity of the appliances they deliver daily, or to achieve 50% better customer reviews in surveys? Measure those metrics before and after training to determine whether your training is delivering the results you need.

- **Make the best decision** about how you will deliver your training. If your franchisees are within a small geographic area and can travel to headquarters, consider delivering live training there, or design training that they will take in a central franchise training center. If your franchisees are working in far-flung locations, you might consider developing training that is delivered to employees' mobile phones or to tablets that you place in every facility. There is no one answer that works in all situations, so evaluate where your employees are, what they do, and make the best decision. Remember that an experienced training development company will be able to help you make the best choices.

The Big Picture

Step back, look at your training as a profit center and ask, "If we had great training, how much would that increase our sales volume? Would it lead to our selling two, three or possibly even more new franchises a year, and what would that be worth to us? If it encouraged our owners to stay with us for longer periods of time, what would that be worth?"

When you crunch the numbers and define the benefits of training, you will see that its value greatly outweighs the cost of doing it right.

Toward the Franchise Operations Manual of the Future

Now, thanks to modern technology, the big thick franchise manuals of the past are disappearing and being replaced with something far better. At Tortal Training, we are tossing aside big printed operations manuals and replacing them with new electronic versions that:

- **Look and function like websites** and are completely interactive.
- **Have content** that is searchable and accessible. If a franchise owner needs immediate information or training on using a franchise's inventory systems, for example, he or she can jump right to that content.
- **Have links to appropriate training embedded** in the manual, right where they belong. If current and future franchisees are consulting the manual about opening a new store, for example, they can jump right to the training programs they need.
- **Interface with a franchise's Learning Management System (LMS),** which tracks exactly who is taking company training, where they are located, whether they have completed their training, earned certification, are selling more, and other key metrics.
- **Can be instantly updated** and enhanced with new or revised content and training options. You can't do that with an old-fashioned printed operations manual. But a

modern electronic manual can evolve and become a living, growing resource for everyone in your franchise system.

- **Can automate the delivery of communications to franchise owners** that can include invitations to take new training courses, to attend your annual franchise conference or regional owners' councils, to be sure to use new signage and displays, and more.

Your Electronic Franchise Manual Can Be Used in Powerful New Ways

For example, Tortal Training is encouraging franchise companies to let prospective new franchise buyers log onto the manual, enroll as users in the franchise's Learning Management System, and take company training. What a powerful way to bring prospective new owners into your franchise family and encourage them to buy.

You can post the names of prospective new owners in a special section of your manual and invite them to take part in training that:

- **Gives a high-level overview** of your franchise's history, products, customers and brand.
- **Covers the basics of what a franchise** is and what responsibilities and

opportunities they will have when they become owners.

- **Gives access to dozens or hundreds of training courses** that let them understand how they will open their locations, merchandise what you sell, use company signage and displays, take part in your marketing programs, hire employees, and be fully supported by your resources and systems.
- **Provides the opportunity to take critical courses** on safety (for all franchises), food safety and preparation (for beverage and food service franchises), and more.
- **Alleviates pre-purchase anxiety** by teaching them about insurance, business finance, and buying or renting real estate to house their franchises.
- **Clearly explains the process** of becoming one of your franchise owners.
- **Parts the curtains** and shows prospective buyers how they will interact with the franchise company. They will attend your annual convention, become part of your franchise councils, and begin an

exciting and successful life as members of your franchise family.

Your Franchise Manual Can Energize Communications Too

We help franchises offer exciting new communications options that can include:

- **Short weekly or monthly podcasts** of key information that are emailed to all current and potential franchisees.
- **Fun games** that work like Jeopardy and other popular game shows that are emailed to all current and potential franchisees.

Long Live the Modern Franchise Operations Manual!

A modern electronic operations manual can increase your franchise's growth and success in ways you never thought possible. It can breathe new life into all your operations, become a powerful sales tool to attract new franchisees, make your current franchisees happier and more committed, and build a franchise brand that engages and delights customers.

Part Twelve:

Sales Training Success

Why Sales Training Should Do More than Get People Fired Up

We recently heard a sales trainer say this to a room full of newly hired salespeople. . .

"Stay fired up! If your prospect throws you out the door, come right back in through the window!"

That piece of advice is like others we have heard over the years, like this one . . .

"If someone hangs up on you, call right back. If it keeps happening, keep calling. You've got to wear some people down before they'll listen to you."

There is a place for advice like that, because selling requires energy, persistence and resilience. But although sales training should be motivational, It should teach some other very important things too, including:

- **A problem-solving mindset.** When your salespeople concentrate as much on solving customers' problems as they do on pitching products and closing sales, they build trust and sell more over time.
- **Deep product knowledge.** Have you ever seen a salesperson who had to page through product manuals to answer the most basic questions about the products he or she was selling? That's a pretty sad spectacle. A salesperson must be able to confidently answer all questions about what he or she is selling.

- **Knowledge of your competition.** To explain the advantages of your products or services, your salespeople must know all about what your competitors are offering.
- **An understanding of how performance will be evaluated**. Will you consider your salespeople successful if they make a certain number of sales calls weekly, close sales on a certain percentage of the calls they make, discover and meet a certain number of new accounts every month, increase the size of previous orders – exactly what, and in what priority? If you fail to set out expectations, you are creating a situation where salespeople are more likely to fall short of expectations and become frustrated and less productive. Another problem? Without specific metrics, how can you measure improvements or judge the performance of your sales team?
- **An understanding of your company history and brand.** Sales techniques and strategies are fine, but your salespeople will make more sales if they can explain what makes your company different from your competitors. Are you grounded in a history of making innovative products or of putting the customer first? Were you founded by a unique leader who has an unusual story or philosophy? Training offers a good opportunity to teach company lore.

Even if you are engaging a training company that offers standardized training packages, find out how much it would cost to add some of the customized features that are outlined above.

Even economical off-the-shelf training should allow for customization.

Are You Asking the Right Questions Before Sales
Training Begins?

Let's consider a common scenario . . .

*Your salespeople aren't selling enough. They're
hitting their quotas by making the number of sales
visits you asked for. They're even identifying and
calling on 20 strong new prospects every month,
just like you asked them to do. But for some reason,
the needle isn't moving in either new client
acquisition or sales dollar volume.*

Who Are You Going to Call?

You call a well-respected sales training company
and hope their instruction can turn things around.
But it is important to be sure that you are getting
to the root causes of problems, not only attacking
the symptoms.

Here are some questions that you should ask, and
then discuss with your training development
company before training begins:

- **Where did we get those sales quotas and
  targets? If they're not working, do they
  make any sense?** If your salespeople are
  hitting your targets but still not selling
  enough, take a step back. Instead of relying
  on training to squeeze more dollars from
  quotas that aren't producing, this is a good
  time to ask whether they are the right ones
  – or even if they make any sense. The next
  question flows logically from this one . . .

- **What are the real reasons sales are not increasing?** Maybe sales are slow because it takes too long to deliver your products or because your customers are unhappy with the customer service you provide. But the underlying question is, will your training try to address underlying causes or attack only the symptoms? Again, the next question flows logically from this one . . .

- **Is the training company you're talking to willing and able to explore underlying big-picture issues, or only trying to bring in a new client?** In the long run, identifying and addressing underlying issues benefits everyone – both you and the training company. That is the kind of training partner you should be looking for.

Train Your Salespeople to Do More than Close Sales

About 90% of sales trainers concentrate on only the moment when salespeople are trying to close sales.

Perhaps that is a good place for trainers to direct most of their attention. But the fact is that salespeople need to be trained on many more skills than just getting an agreement to buy from customers. There are many skills beyond closing that can increase the income-generating abilities of salespeople.

And the good news is, those skills can be trained . . .

- Train your salespeople on **current technologies and trends**. Unless your salespeople are completely up-do-date on them, they cannot adopt the kind of problem-solving role that most customers need today.
- Train your salespeople on what **your competitors** are offering. Without knowing about your competitors' products and what they can do, your salespeople will be unable to sell compellingly.
- Train your salespeople on **the systems** they have to use. The less time your salespeople spend filling out sales reports, filing expense reports and handling other administrative duties, the more time they can spend selling. So . . . train them so they can direct more of their time doing things that

generate income. Another option? Train other employees to handle those tasks so your salespeople can spend more of their time selling.

- Teach your salespeople about your **current marketing and advertising initiatives.** If your salespeople do not know what your marketing wing is doing, they cannot sell effectively. One example? A salesperson was not aware of a current 10% discount that had been announced in the company's website and social media channels. When a customer asked about the discount and the salesperson had not heard about it, that customer became frustrated, and with good reason.

And Finally . . .

Teach your salespeople about your brand! Because they interface with people in the real world every day, they can tell the world about who you are, what you do, and what your brand stands for. They are among your most important brand ambassadors . . . be sure to teach them about your company's history, leaders, values and beliefs.

-

Part Three: Winning Ways to Deliver Great Live Training

- Critical Details and Logistics to Consider for Your Live Training Day
- How to Maximize the Benefits of Classroom Training
- Plan Your Training Day around Energy Highs and Lows
- Include Experiential Learning
- Make Sure Your Training Sessions are the Right Length
- Get More from Training by Assigning the Right Homework
- Resolve Conflicts between Work and Training
-

Part Four: Delivering Great Training at Conferences and Off-Site Meetings

- Plan Off-Site Training that Resonates with Your Company Culture
- Select a Great Conference Venue
- Tips for Choosing and Using the Best Trainers and Speakers
- How to Get the Most from Your Speaker Investment
-

Part Five: What's All This About Metrics?

- Why Training Metrics Matter
- Build Soft Metrics into Your Training Development
- How to Measure whether Your Learners Are Using their New Skills after Training Ends
- What Is the Best Way to Gather Metrics?
- How to Use Metrics to Improve Training

Part Six: Modern Features that Make for Great Training

- Training on Smartphones: Six Critical Questions to Ask Before You Begin
- How Effective Is Social Media for Training?
- The Benefits of Custom eLearning Solutions for Corporate Training
- Why Companies that Train Need to Know about SCORM

Part Seven: Why Your Company Needs Customer Service Training

- Why You Need to Train Your People to Offer Your Customers a Great Experience
- Critical Customer Service Aptitudes that Can Be Trained
- What Kind of Training Works Best to Teach Customer Service Skills?

Part Eight: How to Get the Most Value from Your Learning Management System

- Six Questions to Ask Before You Select an LMS
- Eight Critical Questions to Ask when Selecting an LMS
- How to Get the Most from a Mobile Learning Management System

Part Nine: Secret Sauce Strategies from Our Top Training Designers

- Combine Coaching with Training
- Use the ADDIE Framework to Design Better Training
- Supercharge Your Training by Asking for Feedback from Trainees
- Use Incentives to Boost Training Results

About Tortal Training

Tortal Training specializes in developing interactive eLearning solutions. We make effective training easier by specializing in engagement. We are the only training partner that uses strategic engagement methodologies for organizations with distributed workforces to maximize training effectiveness in an era when talent development is essential in driving sustainable business results.

Call Tortal Training at (704) 323-9053 and speak with a Tortal Training consultant today.

Tortal Training
400 Trade Center, Suite 5900
Woburn, MA, 01801
(704) 323-8953
https://www.tortal.com/

Made in the USA
Las Vegas, NV
23 April 2021